W9-ATT-055

Freedom from Suffering
A Journey of HOPE

Freedom from Suffering
A Journey of HOPE

Developed by
Dr. Stephen F. Grinstead with Ellen Gruber-Grinstead

Foreword by Terence T. Gorski, Endorsement by Dr. Barbara St. Marie

Based in Part on the GORSKI-CENAPS® Model
and the Addiction-Free Pain Management® System

Notice of Proprietary Information: © 1996, 2011 by Dr. Stephen F. Grinstead. This document contains copyrighted and proprietary information of Dr. Stephen F. Grinstead. Its receipt or possession does not convey any right to reproduce it; to disclose its contents; or to manufacture, use, or sell anything it may describe. Reproduction, disclosure, or use without the specific written authorization of Dr. Grinstead is strictly forbidden. If your agency would like the rights to use any part of this material in its program, please refer the appropriate agency representative to: Dr. Stephen F. Grinstead (916) 575-9961, P.O. Box 340626, Sacramento, California, 95834-0626, or e-mail *drgrinstead@yahoo.com* to discuss the arrangements necessary to make that possible. Website: *www.addiction-free.com*.

© 2011 Stephen F. Grinstead

Printed in the United States of America

Additional copies are available from the publisher:
    Herald House/Independence Press
    P.O. Box 390
    Independence, MO 64051-0390
    Phone: 1-800-767-8181 or (816) 521-3015
    Fax: (816) 521-3066
    Website: *www.relapse.org*

For training contact:
    The CENAPS® Corporation
    6147 Deltona Blvd.
    Spring Hill, FL 34606
    Phone: (352) 596-8000
    Fax (352) 596-8002
    E-mail: *info@cenaps.com*

ISBN: 978-0-8309-1512-5   Cover photo: Galina Barskaya|Dreamstime.com

Foreword by
Terence T. Gorski

I have known Dr. Stephen Grinstead for over 20 years. We have worked together in integrating relapse prevention therapy and cognitive-behavioral therapy principles into a comprehensive system for the effective management of chronic pain—*The Addiction-Free Pain Management® System.*

I have suffered for many years from my own chronic pain. During that time I have used many of Steve's suggested methods and found them to be a sanity saver. With his encouragement I have used many of the tools that you will find in this book.

In this new book, *Freedom from Suffering: A Journey of Hope*, Steve has taken his chronic pain management method to a new and even more effective level. He has discussed the dynamics of pain and the techniques for managing it in plain and simple language. This makes his methods even more accessible to those who need it—the people suffering from chronic pain problems and their families and friends.

Any doctor, therapist, or other healthcare professional working with a person suffering from chronic pain can give this book to their patient or patients to help them quickly learn information that would take hours to explain in sessions.

I have a deep respect for Dr. Grinstead as a friend and a colleague. The level of simplicity he brings to the topic as presented in *Freedom from Suffering* is a magnificent accomplishment that will help many.

I especially like the way Dr. Grinstead focuses on the issue of personal responsibility. When we are suffering from a chronic pain problem it affects not only us but those we love and care about. The pain management technology is there, thanks in large part to Dr. Grinstead's work. This gives you the power to exercise your right to effectively manage your pain. You also have a responsibility to those you love and care about to responsibly use this technology so you can build the best possible relationships with your pain and the important people in your life.

I want to close this preface by paraphrasing Dr. Grinstead's words: *Finding freedom from suffering is a journey of hope.* Taking this journey is both your right and your responsibility.

Terence T. (Terry) Gorski
March 2011

Terence T. Gorski is a pioneer in the development of Relapse Prevention Therapy, who has achieved international acclaim for his work. He is considered a leader and authority in the addiction, behavioral health, social services, and correctional industries for his work in recovery and relapse prevention for the past 40 years.

Endorsement by Dr. Barbara St. Marie

Freedom from Suffering: A Journey of Hope should be read by those suffering from pain, those who have loved ones experiencing chronic or persistent pain, and those caring for individuals who suffer from pain. By reading this book you will not feel alone in this experience, and you will obtain an armamentarium of strategies for managing pain.

Dr. Stephen Grinstead has long been a champion and mentor in the field of pain and addiction. This blend of expertise is rare in our society and in healthcare today, but is greatly needed. It is estimated that 76 million people lived with chronic pain in the United States in 2006 (U.S. Department of Health and Human Resources). And, the American Pain Foundation reports that half the individuals who suffer from chronic or persistent pain receive no treatment at all.

It is also estimated that 4.7 million Americans used prescription pain relievers for nonmedical reasons during the month they were surveyed in 2008 (Substance Abuse and Mental Health Services Administration, 2009). This has created many problems not only in healthcare, but also in our society. The very medications that are used to relieve pain may, in some cases, have very detrimental effects in activating the disease of addiction or causing relapse.

When individuals experience addiction and pain there is reluctance with healthcare professionals to prescribe pain treatment, especially opioids. To resolve this tendency, one of the top priorities listed in *Healthy People 2020* (U.S. Department of Health and Human Services, 2009) is to decrease the number of people suffering from untreated pain due to a lack of access to pain treatment. Dr. Grinstead's book, *Freedom from Suffering: A Journey of Hope,* uses a balanced approach to the treatment of chronic or persistent pain, and serves that goal.

Having trained with Dr. Grinstead on managing pain in individuals with the disease of addiction, I have found Dr. Grinstead's lessons and strategies for helping people with pain and addiction very helpful. He provides a guide for balancing medication and nonmedication modalities that has changed my practice. Every health professional has the duty to alleviate pain and suffering, and protect patients from developing addiction or a relapse of their disease. Opioids may or may not be a part of a person's treatment plan for pain, but that does not mean there are no other treatments for their pain. And when opioids are part of the treatment plan, a sensible set of precautions is needed to prevent harm to oneself and others. I continue to use Dr. Grinstead's principles in my daily practice of pain management for people experiencing acute pain, chronic pain, and pain due to life-limiting diseases. These strategies are compassionate, nonjudgmental, and inclusive of the struggles people have while experiencing pain.

Barbara St. Marie

March 2011

Barbara St. Marie, PhD, ANP, GNP, is a certified Adult and Gerontology Nurse Practitioner through the American Nurses Credentialing Center (ANCC). She is certified in Pain Management Nursing through ANCC and in Addiction-Free Pain Management® through Gorski-CENAPS®. She is a graduate of Gustavus Adolphus College in Saint Peter, Minnesota. She has a master's degree in education from the University of St. Thomas in Saint Paul, Minnesota, a master's degree in nursing from the College of St. Catherine in Saint Paul, and is a PhD candidate in nursing at the University of Wisconsin-Milwaukee. She has worked in pain management nursing for over 32 years and has extensively published in the areas of pain and addiction, pain assessment, pain management in the elder patient, and epidural and intrathecal analgesia.

Acknowledgments

First of all I want to appreciate Ellen Gruber-Grinstead, my partner in life and business, not only for her assistance in conceptualizing, analyzing, editing, and formatting this book, but for all her love and support over the past 23 years of our life together.

Writing a book also takes the commitment and cooperation of many people. Although I would like to thank all of the people here who made this book possible that is logistically not possible.

However, there are several people that have helped me who deserve special acknowledgment for making this book possible. I want to thank Terence T. Gorski, founder and president of the Gorski-CENAPS® Corporation, who taught me to conceptualize, analyze, and develop a strategic writing plan that enabled me to bring this book to its final form. I would also like to thank Dr. Jennifer Cory for helping me develop and field-test several components in this book as well as her assistance co-facilitating several of my Addiction-Free Pain Management® clinical skill trainings.

The following people also helped me immensely. Without their outstanding efforts I never would have learned to effectively manage my own chronic pain and this book would not have been possible. Some of the professionals who gave so freely of their own expertise and became a part of my pain management support network are:

- Dr. Kenneth Goranson, an orthopedic surgeon who was willing to support an alternative treatment approach near the beginning of my own journey.
- Dr. Jerry Callaway, a colleague who also consulted on my medication management needs during my early recovery process.
- Dr. Diana Martin, a chiropractor who taught me how to use many valuable pain-reduction tools.

- Ms. Lynn Wiese, a psychotherapist who helped me look at the emotional and psychological components of my own pain and helped me resolve my grieving process.
- I particularly want to thank Miles Roberts, my acupuncturist, and Dr. Katherine Newell, my primary care physician, who helped me manage my latest chronic pain episodes with extraordinary results as I was writing this book.

Finally, I especially want to thank my patients and all of the workshop participants who helped me make *Freedom from Suffering: A Journey of Hope,* more of an experiential rather than an intellectual or academic process.

Most of all, I want to thank my own pain

I now consider the *pain* I live with on a daily basis as a friend. Maintaining a positive relationship with my pain has enabled me to write this book. I offer my experience and my optimism to those who might be feeling hopeless and lost because of their current relationship with pain. Please join me on this journey so you too can experience *Freedom from Suffering*.

Stephen F. Grinstead
April 2011

Contents

Preparing for Your Journey

For the past several years as I have been researching and conceptualizing this book, I have also been dealing with my own chronic pain condition. A series of acute pain flare-ups kept me in bed many mornings, unable to work or participate in normal activities; it had been over 20 years since I felt this kind of intense pain.

It would have been easy to start obsessing about my pain and become depressed as a result. I almost slipped into a "chronic pain trance" and the realization of this motivated me into action. I applied the information covered in this book to myself and began to manage my pain more effectively. I'll talk about this trance state later in the book, but what is important to remember is that this state is an automatic and unconscious way of coping with chronic pain.

In the following chapters you will read about the seven steps that helped me, and the thousands of patients I've worked with over the years, to manage our pain and improve the quality of our lives. You will discover how these steps work and most importantly, how to use them to address your own pain condition. Because of my recent pain flare-ups I had an opportunity to apply a fresh understanding of these pain management tools which made it even easier to explain and detail them in this book.

Living Life to the Fullest as We Face Adversity

I believe that life is meant to be lived to the fullest. For me, the term "fullest" has changed significantly over the past three decades. Before my injury over 28 years ago, my definition included opening my own karate dojo and teaching other people the art I had learned to love with a great passion. I was in my early 30s and believed anything was possible.

After being injured in a construction accident, I lost all hope of ever teaching martial arts again. In fact, I became so depressed I seriously considered ending my life. Today, I'm grateful I didn't give into those feelings of hopelessness and a life of suffering. Instead, I decided to live the best life I could with what I had; this became possible through an intense grieving process that took almost three years. Today I can honestly say I have the life of my dreams and I continue to live it to the fullest.

Develop an attitude of gratitude!

In order for me to live life to the fullest, I must work to maintain an "attitude of gratitude." As I age I am grateful for all the experiences I have had and all the knowledge I have acquired. I'm grateful for all the people who give meaning to my life: my wife Ellen, my mother, friends, colleagues, and especially my recovering brothers and sisters. Instead of feeling depressed about all the things I can't do, I choose to be grateful for all that I can do and everything that is possible.

Aging can also impact our attitudes and how we live life. As we age we may not physically be able to do the things we used to, even if we are not living with chronic pain. But those of us with a chronic pain condition have more challenges to overcome. My karate sensei (teacher), Master Richard Kim, once told us a story about living with adversity that I would like to share with you.

> If you are training and break your toe, be grateful it wasn't your foot. If you break your foot, be grateful it wasn't your leg. And if you break your leg, be grateful it didn't kill you. And if you die, be grateful you don't have to finish this class. The lesson for me was: whenever you hit an obstacle or a difficult time, say "Thank you adversity for yet another test."

As I think of Sensei Kim's suggestion to "thank adversity for yet another test" I realize I have an opportunity to accept my chronic pain condition as one more circumstance to be grateful for and to develop a good plan for managing it successfully.

A major objective of any effective chronic pain management plan, but especially as we age, is an appropriate activity pacing plan. It's important to remember there is a continuum with activity pacing. Our stage of life can become a factor. On one end is the person who always does too much; while on the other end is the sedentary person who does almost nothing.

When developing this activity pacing plan, we must not only pay attention to where we are in the aging process, but also to the limitations our chronic pain condition places in our way. Some of us deny our condition and do too much. We hurt ourselves and then become depressed when we can't do what we want to do. I have been there, and sometimes still go there, so I needed an activity pacing plan that slowed me down.

On the other end some people with chronic pain use aging as an excuse to stop participating in life; they mistakenly believe they can't have a good life because of their condition. These people need more of a jump start, or kick in the butt, to develop an activity pacing plan that encourages them to push more than they normally would.

Stop fighting your pain!

One important suggestion I have for anyone living with chronic pain is to stop making pain your enemy; it's time to make friends with your pain. This can be challenging, but believe me, it's crucial that you make peace with your pain and stop fighting it—pain is part of who you are so you're really just fighting yourself. When you make peace with your pain, you'll be able to create a life worth living filled with meaning and satisfaction.

Today I can honestly say that I'm grateful for that construction accident and my injury. I've found that living with a pain condition for almost three decades has created some limitations for me, but the rewards far outweigh them. I have participated in the healing journey of others living with chronic pain, taught healthcare providers how to work more effectively with their patients suffering with chronic pain, have developed and maintained more fulfilling relationships, as well as writing this book. But my journey did not happen overnight, and neither will yours; it takes commitment, willingness and hope.

Chronic Pain Management Needs More Than a Quick Fix

If you watched any amount of TV the past few years you may have noticed a significant increase in commercials hyping prescription medication. At the same time prescription drug abuse and addiction is on the rise. We live in a quick fix society, so when something goes wrong we look for the fastest and easiest solution.

The Problem: Better Living through Chemistry

When someone has a headache they "pop a pill" and hopefully the headache goes away. When their back starts hurting, finding a medication to deal with the pain is their first and primary concern. The medical system in the United States is second to none in many respects. It is also crisis-oriented and uses symptom management as the first course of action. Taking a pill seems quicker, cheaper, and easier—but is it really? In my experience, people rarely look for the reasons behind their headache or back pain.

What if the pain continues or it becomes a chronic condition? Using certain types of pain medication over long periods of time can cause serious problems. One of the major over-the-counter pain medications used by millions of Americans today is Tylenol (acetaminophen). We now know that acetaminophen can cause liver damage. All medications have side effects, so deciding if they are worth it or not is important to consider.

According to research published in *Pain Physician Journal* (2006), 90 percent of people in the United States receiving treatment for pain management are prescribed opiate medication. Of that number 9 percent to 41 percent experienced opiate abuse or addiction problems. Not only that, prescriptions for medications like Vicodin and Percocet (which both contain acetaminophen) have increased drastically in the past decade, leading to significant medical problems for many people, including addiction.

Because pain is often seen as the enemy, people seeking pain relief want a quick fix. We've been trained by the medical and pharmaceutical industries to expect one. What we have forgotten is that human beings need pain to survive. Pain is the signal that says something is wrong, and as human beings we want to know *why* this something is happening to us. But when it's not possible to pinpoint where pain is coming from, the solution is often symptom management through medication.

Unfortunately, when medication alone does not eliminate the pain or improve the lifestyle losses people are experiencing, the result is usually irrational thinking and uncomfortable emotions—in other words, suffering. The anticipation of an expected level of pain can actually influence the degree to which someone experiences pain.

A person in this situation will say, *this is horrible, awful, and terrible* and then the brain turns up the pain signal. When this happens, the level of distress increases and people suffer, remaining a victim of their pain. This further increases the drive to keep trying one medication after another, or increasing the dose, as the only solution to their pain problem.

The question then that must be asked is: *What can I do now to manage my pain in a healthy way that supports me physically, emotionally, and spiritually?* The answer will be different for each person.

The Solution: A Three-tiered Approach

The search for magical interventions and quick fixes for the treatment of chronic pain can be never-ending. The better option for someone living with chronic pain is to address all the issues with a combination of proven psychological treatment approaches, effective and appropriate medication management, and nonmedication interventions.

Over the past several years, organizations like the International Association for the Study of Pain, the American Academy of Pain Management, and the American Academy of Pain Medicine have all promoted better and safer ways to treat someone undergoing chronic pain management. In fact, they have been advocating many different pain initiatives designed to promote more effective and humane chronic pain management.

For nearly three decades I have assisted people undergoing chronic pain management who were also experiencing coexisting psychological problems including prescription medication abuse or addiction. I've actively helped people in recovery develop more effective—and safer—medication management plans to prevent relapse. I have also worked with people who were living with chronic pain to develop effective medication management plans so they could avoid the risk of prescription medication abuse or addiction.

Finding the safest medication protocol possible cannot be overemphasized; when the narcotic medication is taken in increasingly larger doses due to tolerance, the side effects from the medication may become physically and/or psychologically damaging; in some cases even life-threatening.

Undergoing chronic pain management can be challenging for anyone, but especially for someone with coexisting medication abuse, addiction or other psychological problems. They can become severely depressed and discouraged. Healthcare providers can become confused and frustrated when their treatment interventions are ineffective and will sometimes blame their patients.

The problem of managing pain and medication for people in recovery continues to grow and healthcare professionals are left with the challenge of how to effectively address it. Given the biopsychosocial nature of addiction and chronic pain, it is imperative to understand both conditions and implement a multidisciplinary chronic pain management treatment approach.

Knowledge is power. To that end I have written several books and booklets, as well as published articles and blogs, to get this information out to anyone undergoing chronic pain management. In this book, I emphasize how important it is to understand exactly what you are experiencing in order to effectively manage your pain condition.

When you are in pain you experience both physical and psychological/emotional symptoms. The psychological symptoms include both thinking changes and emotional responses (or uncomfortable feelings) that often lead to suffering. Most people can't differentiate between the physical and psychological types of pain. All they know is: *I hurt!* For effective pain management to occur people need to learn all they can about their pain.

The easiest way to understand pain is to recognize that every time you feel pain, your body is attempting to tell you that something is wrong. Pain sensations are critical to human survival. Without pain you would have no way of knowing that something was wrong with your body and you would be unable to take action to correct the problem or situation that is causing the pain. Whenever you are experiencing pain, it's helpful to ask yourself this question: *What is my pain trying to tell me?*

Psychological treatment for long-term chronic pain conditions is often helpful but as a supplement to medication treatment, not a replacement for it. Emotional stress and negative thinking has been shown to increase the intensity of pain, but the presence of psychological factors doesn't mean that pain is imaginary. Psychological treatment goals are designed to help you learn how to understand, predict, and manage the pain cycle, how to use coping skills to minimize pain, and how to get the most out of active involve-

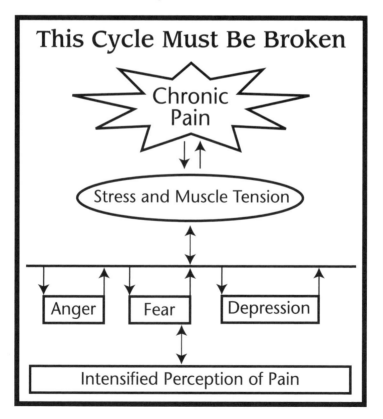

This Cycle Must Be Broken

Chronic Pain

Stress and Muscle Tension

Anger   Fear   Depression

Intensified Perception of Pain

ment in positive life experiences despite the presence of chronic pain.

The chart on page 24 can help you understand the chronic pain cycle.

Being in chronic pain leads to stress and muscle tension. As the stress increases, the body reacts by tensing up and the stress of being in pain increases again; this in turn leads to an additional increase in a person's perception of pain. Here is where the psychological factors come into play. As the chronic pain increases people may get angry, afraid, or depressed. This leads to a further increase in the perception of pain, and the cycle starts again. So how do you break the chronic pain cycle?

The first step to breaking the cycle is to use a combination of physical and psychological interventions. When you implement relaxation response tools, you lessen your stress and muscle tension which will decrease your pain levels. When you use cognitive-behavioral therapy (CBT), which is the process of changing self-defeating thinking and behaviors, your perception of pain also decreases.

Not only that, psychological treatment for chronic pain focuses on the emotional toll on someone living with pain on a daily basis. Important factors such as disability, financial stress, or loss of work are also a part of the pain picture. A psychological treatment plan is needed to address these and other relevant issues.

Although *managing pain without pills* may be a desirable goal, in some cases it may be impossible to achieve, so an "appropriate" medication management plan must be put in place. This plan should be a collaborative process with a professional who understands the biopsychosocial nature of pain and the very real risks of dependency or addiction. In addition to the psychological treatment plan and the medication management plan, implementing non-medication approaches such as acupuncture, chiropractic,

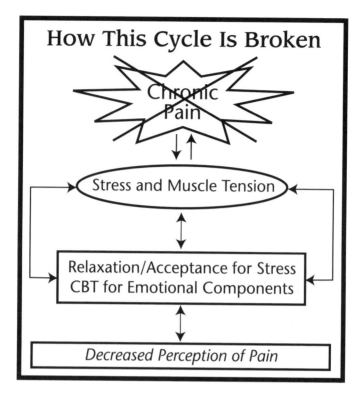

How This Cycle Is Broken

Chronic Pain

Stress and Muscle Tension

Relaxation/Acceptance for Stress
CBT for Emotional Components

Decreased Perception of Pain

massage therapy, hydrotherapy, and biofeedback is vital to an effective pain management plan.

In my early work with patients and my own chronic pain, I realized that chronic pain management required more than a quick fix which is why I developed the Addiction-Free Pain Management® System in 1996.

How This Book Benefits from the Addiction-Free Pain Management® System

This book in based in part on the Addiction-Free Pain Management® (APM) System which is a relapse prevention treatment approach founded on the principles of Terence T. Gorski's biopsychosocial developmental model of recovery. It also integrates the most advanced pain management methods, developed at the nation's leading pain management programs with the most effective treatment methods for addiction developed at the nation's leading addiction treatment programs.

The result is a unique integration of treatment methods that combine cognitive-behavioral interventions and proper medication management along with nonpharmacological (nonmedication based) modalities. The APM™ approach shows patients how to obtain pain relief, while lowering or eliminating their risk of addiction or relapse, as well as reducing or eliminating problems from other mismanaged coexisting conditions.

Since the APM™ system also provides a way to deal with the problem of chronic pain, medication management, and coexisting problems, I believe it is important to include information in this book about potential medication issues.

Freedom from suffering— it's your right and your responsibility!

The predominant focus in *Freedom from Suffering: A Journey of Hope* is intended for those of you living with chronic pain who want to learn and implement seven strategic steps so you can better manage your chronic pain condition, improve your quality of life, stop suffering, and achieve your cherished goals. *Remember that freedom from suffering is your right, but it is also your responsibility!*

You'll manage your pain more effectively when you stop being a passive recipient and start becoming an active participant in your treatment.

In this book you will be asked to examine your personal relationship with your pain and how you manage it, as well as taking an honest look at your medication management plan. The more proactive you are, the more you can improve your ability to manage your pain condition. But you don't have to take this journey alone. This book can also be a valuable tool for people who have friends or loved ones who are coping with a challenging chronic pain condition.

The Role of Family and Friends

Those of you living with chronic pain face obstacles most people will never be confronted with. Some conditions severely limit your level of physical functioning; living with constant pain can also negatively impact your thinking and emotional management ability.

What is often not discussed is the impact on family members and significant others who have to bear witness to the person living with chronic pain. I've seen many families disrupted and marriages end due to mismanaged or poorly managed chronic pain conditions. Sometimes family members and significant others develop their own healthcare problems while trying to help someone they love cope with chronic pain.

Family and significant others often get burned out, or they become frustrated and resentful toward the person living with chronic pain. A spouse can become just as hopeless and helpless as their family member suffering with pain and may even develop a severe depression or sleep problems.

When an individual with chronic pain also develops an addiction problem, family and friends are negatively impacted as with any alcohol or other drug addiction that occurs in a family system. I often refer significant others to Al-Anon or Nar-Anon (Twelve-Step support groups for family and friends of alcoholics or addicts) because they need as much support, if not more, as the person with the addiction.

For those of you who don't have a personal experience of living with chronic pain I want to ask you to follow the steps below to see if you can develop a better understanding of what it is like to live with chronic pain.

Step One: Think back to a time when you hurt yourself or had a painful condition such as a surgery, toothache or headache.

Step Two: Try to remember what that felt like and what you wanted to do to stop the pain.

Step Three: Now imagine that you have that level of pain right now and have had it for the past six months without any relief. Every day when you woke up it was there. Every night you wonder if you'll be able to sleep because the pain is so disturbing.

Step Four: Now imagine trying to explain this to your family and friends or your healthcare provider. What would you say? What would you want from them?

What can friends and family do if a loved one is undergoing chronic pain management, experiencing significant quality of life problems, and a decreased level of functioning? The most important thing is to understand what it must be like; if you answered the four questions above you will have a much better idea. Here are six additional starting points.

1. Make sure you are practicing good self-care; take time to relax, sleep, play, and eat healthy.
2. Develop compassion and even empathy for your significant other—but never sympathy as that can cause even more problems. Remember the old saying "sympathy kills" that is often heard at Al-Anon meetings.
3. Do NOT do things for your significant other that they can and should be doing for themselves.
4. Don't keep secrets from your significant other. This is especially true concerning medication use or abuse issues.

5. Remember the three Cs of Al-Anon: You didn't CAUSE it, you can't CONTROL it, and you can't CURE it.
6. Seek out a professional with experience in pain and addiction for you and your family.

Potential Roadblocks on Your Journey to Freedom

Before looking at ways to overcome the obstacles to freedom from suffering, it is important to explore what those obstacles are in order to develop the best plan possible. But these obstacles are not always easy to see.

The Denial Blindfold

When someone is not aware they have a problem, finding a solution may seem impossible. Many people have a mistaken belief that "I can't be addicted because I'm in pain and besides, my doctor gave me the medication." This can be a type of denial, especially when they have been abusing or have become addicted to their medication. Eventually they will begin to experience life-damaging consequences. If they are in denial, they are unable to see those problems. You'll learn more about this natural and normal human defense system in the next chapter.

Judgmental Healthcare Providers

When chronic pain treatment interventions are ineffective, patients are often blamed for the failure and will receive negative or judgmental messages from their healthcare providers. Many have been told "it's all in your head," "you need to try harder," or "you're making yourself hurt so you can get drugs."

Another phrase often heard from doctors and nurses, as well as mental health and substance abuse counselors, is "they're just drug/med seeking." Before I fully understood the challenges facing people with chronic pain, I also thought some of my patients were "drug seeking." However, I have learned that what they are really looking for is relief from their pain—both physical and emotional. When you think about it, is there anything really wrong with someone wanting relief from their pain?

Unfortunately, negative messages combined with feelings of hopelessness and helplessness can contribute to someone with chronic pain becoming confused, guarded, and defensive. Teaching them how to effectively connect with supportive people is an important part of a recovery program, which will strengthen the prevention of a relapse. This positive support often leads to overcoming confusion and defensiveness.

Tragically, mistaken beliefs about chronic pain and chemical dependency in the healthcare system and recovery community often discourage recovering people from connecting with appropriate support. In fact, misguided advice has often led to life-threatening situations for the person in pain; there have been times when a person following such erroneous advice has died.

I have seen patients with chronic pain and coexisting addiction problems receive completely inappropriate treatment from their healthcare providers. I find these situations very frustrating because they are so unnecessary and can easily lead to a relapse.

One of the biggest roadblocks to effectively managing a chronic pain condition is to not identify and treat coexisting psychological problems, including addiction. In the following section is a brief overview of some of the coexisting problems which will be covered more fully in later chapters.

The Impact of Coexisting Problems

Historically, pain, psychological, and addictive problems have been treated as separate issues. Pain clinics have had success in treating chronic pain conditions. Addiction treatment programs have had success in treating addiction. If the addiction program also treats coexisting problems, their success rate with the coexisting psychological conditions increases as well. Regardless of the effectiveness, pain clinics or addiction treatment programs often fail when the person is suffering with both chronic pain and other coexisting conditions, such as addiction to pain medication.

Within addiction and mental health treatment centers, specific issues need to be addressed in order to obtain positive treatment outcomes for those problems. The same holds true for pain clinics when striving for effective pain management. But, for people who are dealing with coexisting problems, finding appropriate treatment can be difficult and frustrating for them and their healthcare providers—unless their unique treatment needs are adequately addressed.

Dealing with Grief/Loss and Trauma

A major obstacle facing people living with chronic pain is feelings of grief and loss over their prior level of functioning. It's important that a treatment plan is developed to address this issue. Many people with chronic pain and addiction also have a pre-existing trauma history they need to address.

If you have any psychological problem—especially in conjunction with an addiction—and you are not yet fully stabilized, exploring your trauma history could trigger a relapse. It's been my experience that past trauma tends to make a person respond to pain differently, and is often a contributing factor in ineffective pain management and an increased sensitivity to pain signals.

If you do have any unresolved psychological issues, it's important to make sure you resolve your feelings of grief and loss caused by the trauma and chronic pain condition so you can move toward acceptance and reintegrate back into an active, fulfilling life. At this point you should be able to say, and mean it, "today my life is better than ever—it may be different, but it is better and I have hope where before I had none." The goal of the seventh step in this book is to move from merely surviving with chronic pain to thriving.

Anxiety Problems Can Debilitate

Stress is a fact of life, but being "stressed-out" is not. People don't always have control over what happens to them, and sometimes when someone is already worn down by living with chronic pain they can react to challenging situations by feeling overwhelmed, or becoming frazzled or even distraught. Being overly anxious is not only a mental hazard; it's a physical one, too.

The more stressed-out a person is, the more vulnerable they are to colds, flu, and a host of life-threatening or chronic illnesses. As a result, they are often unaware of the beauty and pleasures that living life can bring.

Depression and Isolation

Depression is always a risk for anyone living with under-treated or mistreated chronic pain symptoms. The process starts when a person's thinking and emotions begin to spiral out of control. When their thinking becomes irrational or dysfunctional and they start mismanaging their feelings, they often have urges to indulge in self-defeating, impulsive, or compulsive behaviors to cope with their depression. This in turn affects their relationships with others.

Some people may become isolated and believe they can handle life without any help, or they may become increasingly dependent on others to take care of them, feeling victimized by their pain condition. Either style can worsen their depression. This caretaking by others may enable the depressed person to continue ineffective behaviors and maintain his or her role as a victim.

Some people may need treatment for their depression. An effective depression management treatment plan would include cognitive-behavioral therapy and possibly an anti-depressant medication. Again you'll learn more about the pain depression connection in a later chapter.

How to Get the Most from Your Trance-Breaking Adventure

Adventure? Yes! This can be an exciting adventure, although the word *adventure* may mean different things to different people. I like to define it as: *an unusual or exciting experience.* Another definition may also apply if you aren't careful and prepared for the trip: *an undertaking or enterprise of a hazardous nature.* Because I want to make this adventure—your personal journey—as exciting, freeing, and safe as possible I offer this book as your road map. I want to offer you hope that this adventure is possible as your *journey of hope.*

I can't tell you how many times I've been excited about buying a personal growth or self-help book, but found nothing was much different in my life after reading it. It wasn't the book, but whether or not I put what I read into action. Instead of just "reading" a book, I encourage my patients to treat it like a textbook or instruction manual that they'll be tested on periodically. Why periodically? Many people have learned how to prepare for a test by cramming, but after the test they usually forget most of what they were trying to learn in the first place.

Call to Action

This is why I've incorporated *calls to action* after each chapter and a final call to action at the end of this book. In fact, if you develop more than one action step per chapter, you will increase the benefits you receive. At strategic places within each chapter, I have set up opportunities for you to take time to pause, reflect, and plan.

Imagine you are preparing to go on a trek to a remote

wilderness area that holds many dangerous situations. You would want to have expert guidance from someone who was familiar with the terrain and potential dangers you might face. It would also be good to have help with making your trek comfortable with appropriate supplies and camping equipment. The journey you're embarking on by reading and implementing the action steps in this book is very similar.

You'll Need Guides and Helpers for Your Adventure

To get the most out of this journey, and break through your *chronic pain trance,* you'll want to have guides and other helpers to make it as safe and comfortable as possible. Later in this chapter you'll see how two of my former patients—Mary and Mark—put together their team of guides, coaches, and helpers for their journey to freedom from suffering. As one of your guides, I will be there to help you see the big picture. You will also need to find "local" guides and other helpers that will support you in having a successful journey.

I encourage you to keep a notebook or journal handy while you're reading this book—some of you may want to do this electronically or even use a recorder—whatever works for you is fine. Use the journal to write down your thoughts and experiences when I ask you to reflect on what you've learned.

It's also important that you make a commitment to set aside a specific period of time each day (or for some of you who can't commit to daily, at least three to four times per week) that you will spend reading this book and writing in your journal. It should be at least 30 minutes per sitting, but not more than an hour or two at the most. You may also want to put your "call to action" exercises in your journal rather than writing them down in this book—it's up to you.

Introducing Mary and Mark

In this section I will explain how Mary and Mark broke through their chronic pain trance by taking the information found in this book and putting it into practice. Their names and identities have been modified to protect their confidentiality, but you will see how they found freedom from their suffering by going through this process. Their experiences will help you gain more insight as you complete your own written exercises. As you read about Mary and Mark look for the *similarities* between you and them—not the differences.

I purposely decided to write about two people with fairly serious conditions to demonstrate that this process can help people at this stage, as well as some of you who may not have as serious problems as Mary and Mark do. Although some of you may have even more serious problems, I can assure you that the information in this book certainly won't hurt you, and may very well help in ways you may not expect.

At different points in the following chapters I will also use examples of other patients, and some of my own personal experiences, to help clarify and put a human face on the problem. I will use personal examples when appropriate to show you the challenges I had to overcome on my journey.

Mary's Story

Mary is a 40-year-old married woman with a 19-year-old daughter and a 13-year-old son. She is currently separated from her husband of 20 years as a direct result of how chronic pain impacted her entire family system. Mary was injured on the job in 1999 and diagnosed with two herniated discs in her lower back (L-4/L-5 and L-5/S-1). She underwent surgery in early 2000 that unfortunately made her pain symptoms worse.

Mary was referred to my practice because her doctor

was concerned that she was abusing her pain medication. Her doctor was also concerned that Mary was not benefiting from the multiple pain management procedures she underwent. Some of the procedures included: epidural injections, facet blocks, physical therapy, trigger point injections, and hydrotherapy.

What also complicated Mary's case was the poor response she received from the Workers' Compensation system. Many times needed procedures were not authorized, or were delayed for long periods of time, until her attorney intervened and forced the issue. Her doctors believed that the long delays for some of the procedures contributed to the worsening of her condition. By the time she was finally authorized for treatment, the benefit from them was greatly reduced.

When I first met with Mary she was clinically depressed, using alcohol, and was considering suicide as her only way out. She rated her average level of pain as 9–10 on the 0 to 10 pain scale even with her medications—at the time she was being prescribed 80 mg of OxyContin three times per day and Vicodin 10/660, two to four tablets every four to six hours for *breakthrough pain.*

Mary reluctantly admitted that she had recently also started using alcohol in an effort to escape her pain. Previously Mary had no history of alcohol use, due in part to her strong religious beliefs. She discovered that drinking helped her temporarily escape, but the extreme guilt and shame she experienced as a result contributed to her thinking that life wasn't worth living.

In the following pages you will learn how Mary developed a more effective pain management plan that gave her hope and a better quality of life—a life that she no longer wanted to end. To ensure you get the most out of this book I will show you how Mary (and Mark) completed several parts of the seven steps in this book.

Mark's Story

Mark is a 38-year-old divorced man with a nine-year-old son he lost custody of due to his chronic pain condition and self-defeating behaviors. Mark was injured on the job in 2002 and was diagnosed with a herniated disc in his lower back (L-4/L-5) and one in his cervical area (C-5/C-6). He was working very hard to avoid surgery—he stated that he heard too many "horror stories" about failed surgeries and didn't want to go there.

Mark was referred to my practice because his doctor was concerned about his worsening depression symptoms. Mark's case was complicated by the treatment he was receiving through the Workers' Compensation system due to the industrial accident. Similar to Mary, Mark's procedures, and even medications, were not authorized, or were delayed for long periods of time. It wasn't until his attorney intervened and forced the issue that Mark received the treatment he needed and deserved; although even with legal intervention that wasn't always the case.

When I met with Mark he was so clinically depressed and at such a high risk for suicide, that I initially referred him to a psychiatrist for emergency hospitalization. Fortunately, the hospital placed Mark on appropriate antidepressant medications. He was also authorized to see me for cognitive-behavioral therapy for his depression and pain-focused psychotherapy to help him better cope with his pain.

At our first session after being released from the hospital, he rated his average level of pain as 7–8 on the 0 to 10 pain scale, even with his pain medications. At that time he was being prescribed 75 ug/h Duragesic patch, changed every 48 hours, and Vicodin 5/500, two to four tablets every four to six hours for *breakthrough pain*, as well as one 350 mg tablet of Soma every eight hours. He was still very fragile and reported feeling just as hopeless as when we first started. After working with Mark for several sessions he finally disclosed that he had lost custody of his nine-year-old son.

Mary's Support System (or Guides) and Preliminary Pain Management Plan

I asked Mary to make a list of her professional support system; she included her pain management doctor, the physician assistant (PA) she usually met with, and her Workers' Compensation attorney. She believed that the pain management physician didn't really know her or care about her as she usually met with the PA. She wanted her physician to spend more time with her, but didn't believe that was going to happen. She did think that her PA was on her side and honestly trying to help her better manage her pain, but Mary always wanted more time in their sessions. Although she repeatedly asked for more time and attention, her PA could not honor her request.

When Mary looked at what her attorney was actually doing, she realized that she was not getting the help and answers she needed. She developed a written list of questions that she wanted answered and sent them to her attorney by certified mail. She was very surprised when his office called and set up an appointment to answer her questions.

When I asked Mary to identify her family/friends support system she broke down crying. She had become estranged and isolated from everyone as a result of her chronic pain and depression. She honestly couldn't write anyone down in this area.

I asked Mary to list the medications she was taking for pain management which were OxyContin, Vicodin, and alcohol. She stated that on a 1–10 scale the OxyContin and Vicodin were only giving her a 2–3 level of pain relief that lasted about five hours; if she missed a dose, she experienced withdrawal symptoms and felt even worse. She was beginning to think it wasn't worth taking those medications. She rated the alcohol at a 5–6 level of pain relief, but again it only lasted a few hours and the negative consequences—including severe shame and guilt—far outweighed the benefits she received.

When I asked Mary to list what nonpharmacological (nonmedication or nonmedical) tools she used, she started crying again. She realized that she had stopped using the tools she had learned through physical therapy and hydrotherapy. Mary admitted that she avoided most activities because she believed that if she were active, it would make her pain symptoms worse. She became more hopeful when I mentioned there were some interventions that would help to manage her pain better and get relief.

Mark's Support System (or Guides) and Preliminary Pain Management Plan

When I asked Mark to tell me about his professional support system he listed his pain management doctor, a chiropractor he was also working with, and his Workers' Compensation attorney. He believed that the pain management physician really wanted to help him, but many of the treatment recommendations were not allowed by the Workers' Compensation system.

He did want his physician to spend more time with him, but didn't believe that was going to happen. He also believed that his chiropractor was helping him, especially with his low back pain, but realized sometimes the adjustments worsened his neck pain. One request he came up with for his chiropractor was to reduce the adjustments to his neck.

When he looked at what his attorney had done for him, he realized he was very fortunate compared to other people he knew. He was frustrated, however, when his attorney couldn't get some of the procedures authorized that his doctor believed would make a big difference in managing his pain. I suggested Mark join an advocacy group that was lobbying California lawmakers about the toll Workers' Compensation "reform" was taking on injured workers in the state. This did help him feel more empowered and certainly not alone.

When I asked him to write down all of his family and friends as part of his support system he became very angry. He stated that "nobody cares about me." He had become estranged and isolated from everyone as the result of his anger, chronic pain, and depression. He stated that he honestly couldn't write anyone down in this area. He was willing to work with me to develop a list of people he could count on as you will see in a later chapter.

The medications Mark listed that he was given for pain management included Duragesic, Soma, and Vicodin. He stated that on a 1–10 scale the Duragesic and Vicodin were giving him 4–5 level of pain relief that lasted about six hours, but at times he realized he was overusing his Vicodin because he would forget when he took it. He rated the Soma as only 3–4 level of relief. He was grateful to get the pain relief, but realized that he was experiencing problems with thinking, memory loss, and constipation from the high dose of opiates.

When I asked Mark to list his nonpharmacological pain management tools he admitted he stopped doing several of the stretches and exercises he learned from his chiropractor, and was starting to depend solely on the opiates and Soma for pain relief. He also avoided many daily activities he used to enjoy because he mistakenly believed that if he were excessively active, it would worsen his pain symptoms. He felt more hopeful when he learned there were some activities that would help him to more effectively manage his pain.

Shifting from Hopeless and Helpless
to Freedom from Suffering

As you go through this book you will learn how Mary and Mark transitioned from a hopeless/helpless mindset to a more empowering one. This transition enabled them to manage their pain more effectively and led to a more satisfying quality of life. Again, one of my primary objectives is to periodically share how Mary and Mark—as well as several of my other patients—completed certain steps and eventually obtained their freedom from suffering.

My hope for you is that completing this book becomes a labor of love rather than a burdensome chore. Some sections will go easier than others. Some of you may hit "stuck points" and want to quit. Please don't give in and stop; instead remind yourself that the more you put into the journey, the more you will get out of it. You will learn more about the common stuck points and how to overcome them in the sixth step.

I've tried to make this journey as simple as possible, but that doesn't mean it will be easy. In fact, this may be some of the hardest personal work you have ever attempted, with the biggest personal rewards at the end of it.

Reviewing Your Road Map to Freedom

Congratulations you're just about ready to begin the first step toward learning how to manage pain in a healthier way and gain freedom from your suffering. Below is a brief description of each of the seven steps that will help make your journey successful. This book is designed to be a developmental process—meaning that if you miss or don't fully complete one of the steps, it could cause the effective pain management structure you are building to crumble and crash down around you. My hope is that you will do the work and get the most you can out of this process.

The following seven-step road map is an overview of what you can expect as you embark on your personal journey toward successful pain management.

- **Step One—It's Time to Wake Up:** To begin the journey you will learn about some of the common factors that may be keeping you in a *chronic pain trance*. You'll explore the role of depression and denial and then look at how your thoughts, feelings, and behaviors on bad pain days are negatively impacted. You'll be asked to develop a depression management plan that includes simple ways to address it and break through the chronic pain trance.

- **Step Two—Taking a Fresh Look at Your Relationship with Pain:** In this step you will be asked to take a new look at pain. You will review the pain system as well as the biological, psychological, and social components of a chronic pain condition. You'll see that chronic pain needs to be addressed at three essential levels. We will also look more deeply at three of the roadblocks mentioned above—anxiety, trauma, and sleep problems.

- **Step Three—Exploring Pain versus Suffering:** This is a very crucial step on your journey to true *freedom from suffering.* Part of your success will come from learning the power you have to change your perception of pain and learning how to cope with anticipatory pain. You'll discover how stress management can decrease your levels and perception of pain. You'll also have an opportunity to identify and rate the severity of your pain. I will explain the differences between the physical and psychological/emotional components of pain and show you how Mary and Mark completed that exercise.

- **Step Four—Exploring Effective Pain Management:** At this stage you will examine better ways of getting your chronic pain management needs met. You'll learn about the three core components of an effective pain management plan and be given tips on how to begin developing a personal, proactive, and solid foundation. The three-part approach you'll learn more about is: (1) medication management; (2) cognitive-behavioral treatment; and (3) nonpharmacological interventions.

- **Step Five—To Medicate or Not to Medicate—That *Is* the Question:** In this step you are asked to take an honest look at the medication component of your pain management plan. You'll learn about the Addiction-Pain Syndrome™ and why it's so important to address medication abuse or addiction. You'll also review the definitions of tolerance, dependence, pseudoaddiction, and addiction and learn how to identify the red flags for medication management problems that could sabotage your journey.

- **Step Six—Overcoming the Five Stuck Points to Achieving Full Freedom:** Here you will review the five obstacles that could sabotage your journey and how to successfully move through them: (1) Hopeless to Hopeful; (2) Demoralized to Revitalized; (3) Victim to Victorious; (4) Powerless to Empowered; and (5) Surviving to Thriving.

- **Step Seven—The End of the Beginning:** Like an oldies song once said "you've only just begun." In step seven you will review what you have learned and develop a plan for the next stage of your journey to stay free from suffering. You will also learn about the following five balance points and how to use them as you move forward: (1) Positive Self-Talk; (2) Appropriate Emotional Expression; (3) Healthy Support Network; (4) Spirituality/Humility; and (5) Effective Pain Management.

- **Pulling it All Together:** In this final chapter you will have an opportunity to rate yourself on how much you have accomplished as a result of completing these seven steps to freedom from suffering. You will be amazed at how far you have come.

Call to Action to Prepare for Your Journey

It's time to develop a list of your personal support system (guides and helpers) and your preliminary pain management plan. Again, you can either write in the call to action sections in this book, or record this and future answers in your journal. This information is something you will come back to and refine as you move forward.

Your Professional Guides

To begin, please list all the healthcare support people you are currently working with and answer the following questions about each. If you have more than three, please make sure to answer these questions for them as well.

1. My first professional is: _____
    *   How helpful is this person on a 1–10 scale, with one being not helpful at all to ten being extremely helpful? _____
    *   Why did you rate this person that way? _____
        _____
    *   How could this person be even more helpful working with you? _____
        _____
    *   Are you willing to discuss your needs with them as soon as possible?
        ❑ Yes   ❑ No   ❑ Unsure
        Please explain your answer: _____
        _____
        _____
        _____

2. My second professional is: _____
   - How helpful is this person on a 1–10 scale, with one being not helpful at all to ten being extremely helpful? _____
   - Why did you rate this person that way? _____
     _____
     _____
   - How could this person be even more helpful working with you? _____
     _____
   - Are you willing to discuss your needs with them as soon as possible?
     ❑ Yes   ❑ No   ❑ Unsure
     Please explain your answer: _____
     _____
     _____
     _____

3. My third professional is: _____
   - How helpful is this person on a 1–10 scale, with one being not helpful at all to ten being extremely helpful? _____
   - Why did you rate this person that way? _____
     _____
     _____
   - How could this person be even more helpful working with you? _____
     _____
     Are you willing to discuss your needs with them as soon as possible?
     ❑ Yes   ❑ No   ❑ Unsure
     Please explain your answer: _____
     _____
     _____

Your Helpers—Family/Friends Support

Your next task is to list friends and family members who are currently helping you with your pain management and answer the following questions about each one. If you have more than three, please make sure to answer the following questions about them as well.

1. My first support person is: _____
   - How helpful is this person on a 1–10 scale, with one being not helpful at all to ten being extremely helpful? _____
   - Why did you rate this person that way? _____
   _____
   _____
   - How could this person be even more helpful in supporting you? _____
   _____
   _____

   Are you willing to discuss your needs with them as soon as possible?
   ❏ Yes   ❏ No   ❏ Unsure
   Please explain your answer: _____
   _____
   _____

2. My second support person is: _____
   - How helpful is this person on a 1–10 scale, with one being not helpful at all to ten being extremely helpful?_____
   - Why did you rate this person that way? _____
   _____
   _____
   - How could this person be even more helpful in supporting you? _____
   _____
   _____

Are you willing to discuss your needs with them as soon as possible?

❑ Yes   ❑ No   ❑ Unsure

Please explain your answer: _____

_____

_____

3. My third support person is: _____

   • How helpful is this person on a 1–10 scale, with one being not helpful at all to ten being extremely helpful?_____

   • Why did you rate this person that way? _____

   _____

   _____

   • How could this person be even more helpful in supporting you? _____

   _____

   Are you willing to discuss your needs with them as soon as possible?

   ❑ Yes   ❑ No   ❑ Unsure

   Please explain your answer: _____

   _____

   _____

Exploring Your Current Pain Management Plan

Before we move on to step one, it is essential that you take the time to complete the following exercise and objectively examine your current pain management program. Please be totally honest with yourself here. The point of this exercise is to identify what's working and what's not working with your pain management plan. If you are like some of my patients, you might be taking more than four prescriptions, so be sure to list them as well. Don't forget to include over-the-counter (OTC) medications. Please answer these questions for all additional medications.

Your Current Medication Management Plan

Please list each of the medications you are currently using and answer the questions about each one, including over-the-counter, alcohol or other non-prescribed (legal or illicit) drugs or herbal supplements you may be using.

1. My first medication is _____
   - On a 1–10 scale, with one meaning minimal relief and ten being total relief, how much pain relief do you usually experience with this medication? _____
   - In hours and minutes how long does the relief usually last? _____
   - What, if any, side effects or negative consequences do you usually experience with this medication? _____

   _____
   Are the pain relief benefits worth any negative effects?
   ❑ Yes ❑ No ❑ Unsure
   Please explain your answer: _____

   _____
   _____

2. My second medication is _____
   - On a 1–10 scale, with one meaning minimal relief and ten being total relief, how much pain relief do you usually experience with this medication? _____
   - In hours and minutes how long does the relief usually last? _____
   - What, if any, side effects or negative consequences do you usually experience with this medication? _____

   _____
   Are the pain relief benefits worth any negative effects?
   ❑ Yes ❑ No ❑ Unsure
   Please explain your answer: _____

   _____

3. My third medication is _____
   - On a 1–10 scale, with one meaning minimal relief and ten being total relief, how much pain relief do you usually experience with this medication? _____
   - In hours and minutes how long does the relief usually last? _____
   - What, if any, side effects or negative consequences do you usually experience with this medication? _____
   _____
   _____

   Are the pain relief benefits worth any negative effects?
   ❑ Yes ❑ No ❑ Unsure
   Please explain your answer: _____
   _____
   _____

4. My fourth medication is _____
   - On a 1–10 scale, with one meaning minimal relief and ten being total relief, how much pain relief do you usually experience with this medication? _____
   - In hours and minutes how long does the relief usually last? _____
   - What, if any, side effects or negative consequences do you usually experience with this medication? _____
   _____
   _____

   Are the pain relief benefits worth any negative effects?
   ❑ Yes ❑ No ❑ Unsure
   Please explain your answer: _____
   _____
   _____

Your Nonpharmacological Interventions

In this section please list any nonmedication or nonmedical type pain management tools that you are currently utilizing. These can include chiropractic, acupuncture, biofeedback, physical therapy, ice/heat, exercise, stretching, yoga, and hydrotherapy. You will be given an opportunity in a later section to modify or enhance this preliminary list of nonpharmacological interventions. As before, if you have more than four nonpharmacological interventions, please list them and answer the following questions for those as well.

1. My first intervention is _____
   - On a 1–10 scale, with one meaning minimal relief and ten being total relief, how much pain relief do you usually experience with this intervention? _____
   - In hours and minutes how long does the relief usually last? _____
   - What, if any, side effects or negative consequences do you usually experience with this intervention? _____
   _____
   Are the pain relief benefits worth any negative effects?
   ❏ Yes ❏ No ❏ Unsure
   Please explain your answer: _____
   _____
   _____

2. My second intervention is _____
   - On a 1–10 scale, with one meaning minimal relief and ten being total relief, how much pain relief do you usually experience with this intervention? _____
   - In hours and minutes how long does the relief usually last? _____
   What, if any, side effects or negative consequences do you usually experience with this intervention? _____
   _____
   Are the pain relief benefits worth any negative effects?
   ❏ Yes ❏ No ❏ Unsure
   Please explain your answer: _____
   _____

3. My third intervention is _____
   - On a 1–10 scale, with one meaning minimal relief and ten being total relief, how much pain relief do you usually experience with this intervention? _____
   - In hours and minutes how long does the relief usually last? _____
   - What, if any, side effects or negative consequences do you usually experience with this intervention? _____

   _____

   Are the pain relief benefits worth any negative effects?
   ❑ Yes   ❑ No   ❑ Unsure
   Please explain your answer: _____

   _____
   _____

4. My fourth intervention is _____
   - On a 1–10 scale, with one meaning minimal relief and ten being total relief, how much pain relief do you usually experience with this intervention? _____
   - In hours and minutes how long does the relief usually last? _____
   - What, if any, side effects or negative consequences do you usually experience with this intervention? _____

   _____

   Are the pain relief benefits worth any negative effects?
   ❑ Yes   ❑ No   ❑ Unsure
   Please explain your answer: _____

   _____
   _____
   _____
   _____

**Now You're Ready to Start Step One
on the Next Page**

Step One:
It's Time to Wake Up

The Nature of the Beast

Today, chronic pain is one of the most critical healthcare issues in the world. In the United States alone, more than 100 million people suffer with some type of chronic pain—affecting one in five Americans. Chronic pain takes its toll on personal lives, healthcare resources, and the economy. According to *Health & Productivity Management Journal* 2:2 (2005), chronic pain accounts for more than $100 billion in medical expenses and more than $70 billion each year in lost productivity, unsafe working conditions, and increased absenteeism.

All over the world many people living with chronic pain are not receiving timely and appropriate treatment interventions. For some of them it's because they don't have medical insurance or the ability to pay for the services they desperately need. Others belong to managed care or HMOs that restrict services. Still others may be victims of the Workers' Compensation system that assumes they are faking the severity of their injury or trying to defraud the system.

I believe that healthcare services and especially chronic pain management should be a right, not a privilege. In 2004 during the *Global Day Against Pain* the World Health Organization (WHO) and the International Association for the Study of Pain (IASP), along with many other organizations, issued a joint declaration stating that "The Treatment of Pain Should be a Human Right." These organizations released research documents demonstrating that the management of pain has been a neglected area of many governments in the

53

developed world despite the fact that cost-effective methods of pain control are readily available.

The IASP recently released the results of a systematic review of the literature regarding the relationship between waiting times, health status and health outcomes for patients needing treatment for chronic pain. Twenty-four studies met the inclusion criteria for the review. Despite the differences across studies, the results indicated that wait times of six months and over for the treatment for chronic pain are associated with deterioration in health-related quality of life and psychological well-being, including an increase in depression scores.

In the United States, it is necessary for hospitals to comply with pain management standards put in place by the Joint Commission on Accreditation of Healthcare Organizations (JCAHO) in 2001. However, it is now mandated that addiction treatment and mental health centers that are accredited by JCAHO also adhere to these pain management standards which require healthcare providers to:

- Recognize the right of patients to receive appropriate assessment and management of pain.
- Establish the existence of pain and assess its nature and intensity in all patients.
- Record the results of the assessment in a way that facilitates regular reassessment and follow-up.
- Determine and assure staff competency in pain assessment and management, as well as address pain assessment and management in the orientation of all new staff.
- Establish policies and procedures which support the appropriate prescription or ordering of effective pain medications.
- Educate patients and their families about effective pain management.
- Address patient needs for symptom management in the discharge planning process.

I have found that many addiction and coexisting disorder treatment programs do not appropriately adhere to these standards, due to the mistaken belief that when someone is in addiction recovery they should not take anything—no matter what! In addition, many treatment programs do not fall under the jurisdiction of JCAHO and therefore have no pain management standards to adhere to.

Below is my *Seven Point Clinical Philosophy of Pain Management* that I developed for our Addiction-Free Pain Management® Centers of Excellence in the United States. I modified this list for pain specific programs. I would like to suggest that all treatment programs and pain management practices develop similar strength-based philosophies for effective pain management.

1. We believe that each patient's report of pain is valid. Our approach to assisting the patient is driven by this basic assumption.
2. We treat each patient with dignity, acknowledging their perception of pain and accepting their cultural, spiritual, and psychological values as their reality.
3. Our primary goal is to assist the patient in wisely and skillfully managing their pain experiences, based on the patient's stated desire for pain relief.
4. We will work diligently to complete a comprehensive pain assessment with reassessment at regular intervals taking into account a patient's progress. This can only be accomplished using a multidisciplinary team approach.
5. Effective pain relief will be a primary component of the patient's interdisciplinary treatment plan. We educate all clinicians to assure competence in dealing with patients whose treatment is complicated by coexisting problems including addiction.
6. Our role is that of advocate for the patient to assist him/her in achieving their quality of life goals while providing relief of pain.

7. We have a protocol in place for ongoing examination of our work treating patients with acute and/or chronic pain. If we determine that we are unable to adequately and safely treat a patient with chronic pain and co-occurring issues, we will offer resources to the patient that may better address his or her pain management needs.

The Chronic Pain Trance

As I mentioned in my introduction, people living with chronic pain sometimes develop an automatic and unconscious way of coping with chronic pain that I call the *chronic pain trance*. For some people this means adopting a hopeless/helpless mindset and mistakenly believing their life is over. Others try to cope with their situation by embarking on a quest to find the right *pill*, while still others try to find someone to *rescue* or *fix* them. If you are stuck in your own *chronic pain trance,* you can learn to avoid these self-destructive coping mechanisms. You have a responsibility to yourself and those who care about you to break through this trance.

The chronic pain trance is a dark and difficult place, as you saw earlier when Mary and Mark didn't receive appropriate treatment early on. Pain, especially chronic pain, is an emotional condition as well as a physical sensation. It is a complex experience that affects thought, mood, and behavior and can lead to isolation, immobility, and sometimes drug dependence or addiction. A quick response is necessary to lessen the risk of these life-threatening consequences.

Reveille—it's time to wake up!

I remember my days in the Marine Corps when every morning we woke up with a bugle playing "reveille," which comes from the French word for "wake up." If only waking up from the *chronic pain trance* was as simple as responding to a bugle call.

From Despair to Hope:
A Recovery Story

Living with chronic pain is very challenging. If a person also has coexisting problems, including addiction, it makes recovery even harder. Many people who have chronic pain and coexisting problems become very depressed and feel hopeless. They have often lost their self-esteem and the support of significant others, who may be feeling burned out by trying to be overly helpful. Healthcare providers often become confused and frustrated when none of their treatment interventions seem to work.

Sometimes it's helpful to put a face on this painful situation, so let me introduce you to Jerry. When I started working with him, Jerry was a 34-year-old, married man with a wife and three teenage children. Three years earlier he was injured in a construction accident and had been unable to work not long after his injury. At first Jerry was very hopeful that he would be able to return to work in a short period of time and believed that everything would be fine. Unfortunately, that's not what happened.

Although his injury was very painful and he had great difficulty even walking, his treating physician determined—without appropriate diagnostic testing—that Jerry was "only" suffering from severe muscle strain and prescribed analgesic narcotics and antispasmodic (muscle relaxation) medication.

Jerry attempted to return to his job on limited duty and tried his best to cope with the increasing pain symptoms, but found it harder and harder to keep going. After two months Jerry sought legal counsel and discovered that he had the right to seek another doctor. This began a three-year journey of confusion and frustration.

The new doctor he chose ordered diagnostic testing, including a magnetic resonance imaging (MRI) scan and computed tomography (CT) scan, which determined that he had three damaged discs in his lower back. The doctor immediately referred Jerry to an orthopedic surgeon to discuss treatment alternatives. Jerry was very frightened, but at the time refused to let anyone know how terrified he really was.

After a brief physical examination and review of Jerry's diagnostic test results, the surgeon recommended an extensive surgical procedure. The doctor told Jerry that without the surgery he could end up being paralyzed, or at best, continue to live in excruciating pain. The consultation session was very brief and Jerry got the impression that the doctor wasn't really listening to his concerns. He felt rushed into making a decision, but because he had so much distress around his pain he reluctantly agreed to the surgery.

During the next three years Jerry had four surgeries. By the time I started working with him the surgeries Jerry had contributed to his pain becoming worse, instead of getting better. His surgeon declared the surgeries "successful," and there was nothing more he could do for him. He discharged Jerry and referred him to a pain clinic.

After an extensive assessment procedure at the pain clinic, it was determined that Jerry could be helped, but it would take hard work and the implementation of an integrated multidisciplinary treatment plan. The pain clinic referred Jerry to me in order to assess his physiological and psychological/emotional pain symptoms, to consult on his medication management, and to recommend a multidisciplinary treatment protocol.

During my evaluation I discovered that Jerry had physiological and psychological/emotional pain symptoms. The psychological/emotional symptoms were more predominant which turned out to be a good prognosis for Jerry's eventual recovery. I also determined that Jerry had become addicted to his pain medication and was experiencing significant negative consequences as a result.

Jerry had a difficult time accepting that he had become addicted. After all, he did have a serious chronic pain condition and doctors had prescribed the medication. I listened to Jerry and validated his concerns. Eventually he began to trust me enough to begin looking at the emotional pain he was experiencing around the trauma of the past three years. He realized that he was using his pain medication to escape those emotions.

Together with his doctor at the pain clinic, we developed a more effective medication management plan that included epidural and trigger point injections coupled with nonmedication interventions such as hydrotherapy and massage therapy. At the same time Jerry and I started working on a psychological and emotional pain management plan, as well as developing a recovery plan for his addiction using the *Addiction-Free Pain Management® (APM) Recovery Guide* and the *APM™ Workbook*.

It was not easy for Jerry; there were many days that he wanted to give up and he even considered suicide. Jerry had developed severe clinical depression due to his injury, the multiple surgeries, and his significantly decreased quality of life. His depression needed to be addressed immediately. I asked his doctor to consider an antidepressant medication while I worked with Jerry using cognitive-behavioral therapy interventions. After four or five weeks his depression symptoms had significantly improved. This was a real turning point in Jerry's recovery and pain management process.

After three years Jerry finally began the shift from despair to hope. He was learning that although he may need to live with chronic pain, he no longer had to suffer with it. He even learned to communicate his feelings more effectively and started reconnecting with his family in a much healthier way. By continuing with his recovery and pain management plan, Jerry was able to experience a more positive quality of life.

In some ways the *chronic pain trance* resembles depression in that the relationship between the two is very intimate. Living with chronic pain is depressing, and depression can cause and even intensify pain. People living with chronic pain have three times the average risk of developing coexisting psychological problems—usually mood or anxiety conditions—and depressed people have three times the average risk of developing chronic pain.

Depression Can Sabotage Chronic Pain Management

Clinical depression is the number one psychological condition that causes the biggest problems for the most people living with chronic pain—and it often gets underdiagnosed and/or undertreated. A variety of recent medical studies have drawn a strong association between chronic pain and the diagnosis of major depression. The two conditions seem to go hand-in-hand in a large percentage of people who suffer the debilitating effects of both chronically painful conditions and persistent mood problems.

Researchers still cannot determine whether there is a cause-and-effect relationship between chronic pain and depression, and if there is, which condition causes the other. Some research suggests that insufficiently treated, ongoing pain may cause changes in the chemical environment of the brain, thereby increasing the likelihood of depression. Similarly, other research suggests that insufficiently treated, ongoing depression can cause changes in the chemical environment of the brain such that it increases an individual's perception of painful sensations. Regardless of what came first, concurrent treatment is necessary for successful treatment outcomes.

The Depression Barrier

There are several types of clinical depression that involve disturbances in mood, concentration, self-confidence, sleep, appetite, activity, and behavior as well as disruptions in friendships, family, work, and school. Clinical depression is different from the experience of sadness, disappointment, and grief familiar to everyone and can sometimes make it difficult to determine when professional help is necessary.

The following information will provide you with a brief overview of the symptoms, causes, and treatment of clinical depression. It also includes tools to help assess the severity of any symptoms you may be experiencing in order to determine whether you should consider developing a depression treatment plan at this time.

Feeling Down versus Being Depressed

A period of depressed mood that lasts for several days or a few weeks is often just a normal part of life and is not necessarily a cause for concern. Although these feelings are often referred to as *depression,* they typically do not constitute a clinical depression since the symptoms are relatively mild and only last for a short period of time. Moreover, milder periods of depression are often related to specific stressful life events and improvement frequently coincides with the reduction or elimination of the stressor—this is referred to as *situational depression.*

A person with clinical depression, however, experiences substantial changes in their mood, thinking, behaviors, activities, and self-perceptions. A depressed person often has difficulty making decisions, for example, and the day-to-day tasks of paying bills, attending classes, reading assignments, and returning phone calls may seem overwhelming.

A depressed person may also dwell on negative thoughts, focus on unpleasant experiences, describe themselves as a failure, report that things are hopeless, and feel as though they are a burden to others. The changes in mood brought on by depression frequently result in feelings of sadness, irritability, anger, emptiness, and anxiety and may even lead to thoughts of suicide.

There are also different types of depression, including bipolar disorder, in which depressive episodes alternate with manic or hypomanic episodes which may include feelings of agitation and euphoria. A severe or long-term depressive episode can substantially wear down self-esteem and may result in thoughts of death and even attempts at suicide.

The combination of depression and pain is reflected in the circuitry of the nervous system. In the experience of pain, communication between body and brain goes both ways—in a future chapter I'll discuss the ascending/descending pain phenomenon in more depth. Normally, the brain diverts signals of physical discomfort so we can concentrate on the external world. When this shut-off mechanism is impaired, physical sensations, including pain, are more likely to become the center of attention.

Brain pathways that handle the reception of pain signals, including the seat of emotions in the limbic region of the brain, use some of the same neurotransmitters involved in the regulation of mood, especially serotonin and norepinephrine. When that regulation is impaired or fails, pain is intensified along with sadness, hopelessness, and anxiety. And chronic pain, like chronic depression, can alter the functioning of the nervous system and perpetuate itself.

We know that pain is a signal that tells us there is damage or there is something wrong with our system. However, the system (including the brain) can be altered with some chronic pain conditions. The pain system gets turned on and cannot be turned off. This is a major reason why many people living with chronic pain slip into a chronic pain trance.

Over, Around, or Through the Depression Barrier

One of the biggest challenges of treating depression in

people with chronic pain is missing the diagnosis in the first place. This occurs for two reasons: (1) the person in chronic pain often does not realize he or she is also suffering from a major depression; and (2) the doctor is not looking for it. People living with chronic pain will often define their problem as strictly medical and directly related to their pain. Therefore, exploring whether or not depression is present and being willing to develop a treatment strategy, becomes a crucial component of an effective pain management treatment plan.

If symptoms related to a depressive condition are interfering with your ability to do routine, day-to-day activities, then you should consider seeking professional help. There are a variety of highly effective interventions available for the treatment of depression.

The majority of depressive conditions can be treated with either psychotherapy (especially cognitive-behavioral therapy) or medication, but research studies indicate that a combination of these interventions is usually the most effective form of treatment. There are also some types of depression that have a seasonal pattern where intensive *full-spectrum lighting* therapy is often effective in reducing symptoms. It should be emphasized that the majority of depressive conditions can be treated without hospitalization.

Medication + Psychotherapy Is Considered the Most Effective Treatment

If you seek treatment, the recommendations you receive will likely depend on the specific symptoms you have experienced, their duration and severity, and any previous history of depression. As you consider your treatment options, you should assess the relative costs and benefits of different forms of treatment. For example, there are possible side effects associated with antidepressant medications, but these medications can be a very effective and expedient form of treatment.

Frequently, psychotherapy can be a very useful way of resolving emotional and interpersonal problems associated with depression, but it does require a commitment of your time and energy. All of the depressive conditions are highly treatable and many individuals experience a full recovery from their symptoms. You are encouraged to discuss any questions or concerns you may have about treatment with a counselor or physician.

Helping Yourself

The first step toward helping yourself is to identify the emotional, psychological, and behavioral symptoms you have been experiencing which may be related to depression. You should also assess how depression is impacting other areas of your life, including relationships with family and friends, finances, and academic or work responsibilities. Discussing these problems with the people involved or with an understanding friend, may resolve some of the issues before the depression becomes more serious. You may also want to consider the following:

Common Depression Management Tools

Things to Do When You're Depressed

- Eliminate the use of alcohol and other drugs (other than appropriate prescriptions)
- Exercise or engage in some form of physical activity every day, such as walking
- Eat a proper, well-balanced diet and take a good multivitamin daily
- Make sure to get an adequate amount of sleep. If sleep is a problem, discuss this with your doctor/therapist
- Seek emotional support from friends and family
- Focus on positive aspects of your life

- Pace yourself, modify your schedule, and set realistic goals
- Eliminate or reduce unnecessary tasks so your schedule is more manageable
- Reduce or eliminate the use of nicotine, caffeine, and sugar
- Consult with a physician if you are experiencing any medical problems
- Consult with a dentist if you are experiencing any dental problems
- Seek early intervention which may improve the severity of your depression

Things to Avoid When You're Depressed

- Isolating
- Making long-term commitments or important decisions unless absolutely necessary
- Overcommitting to activities which are too stressful or overwhelming
- Assuming that life challenges are hopeless—they're not!
- Engaging in *emotional reasoning* (for example, "because I feel awful, my life is terrible")
- Assuming responsibility for events that are outside of your control
- Avoiding treatment as a way of coping
- Pushing people away who try to help you

Helping a Depressed Friend

If you recognize depression symptoms in yourself, it's important to seek social support in addition to medical and psychological help. However, you also need to teach people how to help you when you're feeling depressed.

Some of you reading this have friends or loved ones who are experiencing depression. Maybe you've asked yourself "How can I help?" Some of you may have become frustrated, fearful, anxious, or even angry with the depressed person, and you may even want to escape or avoid them. If someone you care about is struggling with depression, you can be a valuable resource. Or, if you are living with depression, you can share this information with your support team.

A depressed individual can be emotionally withdrawn, isolated, lethargic, self-critical, and sometimes suicidal. If you talk candidly with them about your concerns for their well-being, it will often bring the problems out into the open. Emphasize that your primary objective is to convey feelings of concern and assist them in receiving appropriate, professional help. If they express thoughts of suicide, but refuse to seek help, you should speak with a mental health professional. I would also highly recommend the book, *Straight Talk about Suicide,* which was published in 2010 by Terence T. Gorski.

Following are some examples of things others can do. Please have your family and friends read this next part so they can be more supportive of what you are going through.

Suggestions for Helping a Depressed Friend

- Instead of trying to *cheer them up*, be empathic and understanding
- Refrain from using critical or shaming statements
- Refuse to engage in expressions of hopelessness or argue about how bad things are
- Empathize with their feelings of sadness, grief, anger, and frustration
- Resist the urge to convince them that depression or sadness are the *wrong* feelings
- Redirect your anger when your efforts are resisted or rejected
- Advocate and push for recovery from depression

- Emphasize that depression is treatable
- Seek help if a depressed friend refuses necessary treatment

Many people with chronic pain frequently become depressed due to living with undertreated or mistreated chronic pain symptoms. The depression process starts when thinking and emotions begin to cause problems. When thinking becomes irrational or dysfunctional you start mismanaging your feelings, and often have urges to indulge in self-defeating, impulsive or compulsive behaviors to cope with your depression. This in turn affects your relationships with others.

The Pitfalls of Isolation and Enabling

Some of you may become isolated and believe you can handle your problems without any help, or you may become increasingly dependent on others to take care of you. Either style can worsen your depression and increase your need for treatment. In addition, this caretaking by others may enable you to continue ineffective behaviors and help maintain your role as a victim.

Research indicates that effective treatment includes a combination of medication and therapeutic interventions.

An effective depression management treatment plan includes cognitive-behavioral therapy and possibly antidepressant medication which have been proven to be the most effective treatment for depression and may need to be a crucial component of your pain management plan.

Mary's and Mark's Initial Depression Management Plans

Mary and Mark reviewed the same information on depression that you just covered. After reviewing it and asking several questions, they both developed their initial six-part depression management plan. I explained to them that many of the interventions they chose would not only help them with depression, but also improve their pain management.

Mary's Depression Management Plan

- Mary's first step was to follow my recommendation for evaluation by a psychiatrist for antidepressant medication. She was prescribed a selective serotonin reuptake inhibitor (SSRI). This medication was prescribed not only for its antidepressant properties, but because it also helps people better cope with their chronic pain symptoms. Her doctor explained that it could take four to seven weeks for it to take full effect and that she needed to work on other cognitive-behavioral depression management interventions in the meantime. Mary believed this was important because she did not like feeling depressed and suicidal. She did not see any obstacles that would prevent her from taking her medication and felt more hopeful knowing she was getting into action.

- Her second intervention was to immediately stop using alcohol and to start eating a healthy balanced diet including nutritional supplements. She saw fear and craving as major obstacles in adhering to this intervention and was willing to commit to going to Alcoholics Anonymous (AA) meetings, as well as asking her minister for additional spiritual support with stopping her alcohol use.

- Her third intervention was to decrease her isolation tendencies. She planned to use both AA and her church activities to help her achieve this goal. She knew that she would be tempted to continue isolating; to help her overcome this self-defeating pattern she developed a support network and asked them to call her every day if she didn't call them first. Some of the people she chose were from her AA meetings and others were from her church group.

- The fourth activity that she believed was important to include was listening to the self-hypnotic cassette tape I gave her called *Up from Depression.* She admitted that procrastination could sabotage following through with this, so she decided to make small colorful posters by her bed and also by her favorite chair that would remind her to stop and listen to her tape.
- At first Mary complained that she couldn't think of anything else, but was willing to engage in a brainstorming session with me to see what else we could come up with together. As a result, her fifth intervention was to set better limits and boundaries with her family and friends regarding how much physical activity she could tolerate. She cited low self-worth and guilt/shame as major obstacles to making this happen. To help her, we agreed to role-play different ways for her to ask to get her needs met and for her to come up with several reasons why she deserved to take care of herself.
- Mary's final intervention was to keep a daily gratitude journal. This was a great way for her to focus on the positive aspects of her life instead of only seeing what was bad. Again she listed procrastination as the major obstacle; to help overcome that she purchased a very nice journal she kept on the nightstand by her bed. Making a gratitude list was the last thing she did before turning off the light and going to sleep.

Mark's Depression Management Plan

- Since he was already taking two different types of antidepressants when he was discharged from the hospital, Mark believed it was crucial that his first intervention include ways to prevent this situation from ever happening again. His psychiatrist decided that a combination of Wellbutrin and trazadone would be the most helpful for Mark. The doctor explained that the trazadone would also help him with sleep—Mark had only been sleeping two to three hours per day for several months. Mark knew that he had a tendency to be forgetful about taking his medications as prescribed, so he needed to address this. The plan he developed was to purchase a weekly plastic pill sorting case from his pharmacy; every Sunday night he would put his medications in the various trays. The trays had daily bins as well as morning, afternoon, and evening trays which helped him adhere to his medication management plan.

- Mark decided that he needed to develop a much better diet and to reduce his nicotine and caffeine intake. He had learned the importance of good nutrition since he had already lost a significant amount of weight. He identified procrastination as a major obstacle toward implementing his plan. To help overcome this he signed up for a weekly diet/nutrition class offered by the hospital he was at. He also learned to implement weekly meal planning menus and shopping lists. He joined a free smoking cessation program sponsored by the local YMCA and started drinking decaffeinated coffee. To help him succeed with all of these interventions, he committed to checking in about his progress or difficulties he was having at the beginning of each of our weekly sessions.

- Mark realized he needed to address his isolation tendencies and start reaching out more. He knew that loneliness was a major contributing factor to his feeling suicidal; he was clear that he never wanted to go through that again. He decided one of the steps he wanted to take was signing up for a parenting class. This would help him with reunification with his son and seeking joint custody. He also agreed to family therapy sessions to help his son heal from the trauma of the divorce and the bitter custody battle. He also decided to join the local Parents Without

Partners support group which also offered activities that he could participate in with his son.

- Mark committed to implementing a physical exercise regime after learning that exercise would not only help with his depression management, but improve his pain management as well. One obstacle he foresaw was a tendency to overexercise, which in the past led to major pain flare-ups. To help him achieve this goal he consulted with his doctor and chiropractor to develop a written list of daily exercise and stretching activities that was designed to increase mobility and flexibility, as well as to build muscle. Mark took one additional step to assure his compliance with this plan; he created a large collage reflecting his intention to achieve and live a much higher quality of life—he had it framed and hung it in his living room as a constant reminder. He knew that improving his physical fitness would help him achieve his goal.

- Mark's fifth depression management activity was to commit to being proactive with the *cognitive restructuring* interventions I offered to teach him. His first assignment was to keep a daily journal listing all of the depressed or irrational thoughts that surfaced each day. He then was to come up with two to three positive challenges to each of those negative-thinking patterns. He saw procrastination and his poor memory as potential obstacles to following through. To help overcome those roadblocks, he purchased a special hardcover journal that he would keep on his nightstand and write in every night before turning off the lights for sleep. He also committed to share with me what worked and any problems he experienced during each of our sessions, as well as giving me permission to challenge him when he failed to follow through.

- Mark's final approach was to set daily personal and social goals. Mark admitted that he had not had enough motivation to set daily goals for a long time. He knew that

71

apathy and his depressed thinking could easily distract him from being successful at setting and reaching daily goals. To help overcome this he made a commitment to call his best friend every morning to share his goals and at the same time he would share his progress or difficulties with the previous day's goals. He agreed to keep a written record of his goals and bring a copy to each of our sessions as further insurance that would help hold him accountable in accomplishing them.

Your Personal Depression Management Plan

Now that you have reviewed all the above information about depression and have had a chance to review Mary's and Mark's plans, it's time to put your new knowledge and understanding to practical use. You will now have an opportunity to develop your own depression management plan. Remember, when you effectively treat your depression, you will also be helping your pain management.

Review the sections above on medication interventions, things to do, and things to avoid. Then using that as a starting point, as well as reviewing what Mary and Mark did, please write down your step-by-step action plan in your personal journal—your plan should have at least six (6) steps. If you are depressed, one of the steps should be setting up an evaluation to make sure it is not a medical condition that is causing the depression, and being willing to consider appropriate treatment that may include antidepressant medication if recommended.

> **Please Take the Time Now to Develop Your Depression Management Plan in Your Journal**

72

Neuroplasticity and the Chronic Pain Trance

The science of neuroplasticity is complex and not easily understood. In essence, the brain forms pathways called neuronetworks that eventually become superhighways—in other words the newly developed neuronetwork becomes even more complex and elaborate.

A surprising consequence of neuroplasticity is that the brain activity associated with a given function can move to a different location as a consequence of normal experience or brain damage/recovery. In the case of chronic pain, this can mean that pain signals keep occurring despite lack of a trigger or tissue damage.

According to research published in *Annals of the New York Academy of Sciences* (2001) titled "Spinal Cord Neuroplasticity following Repeated Opioid Exposure and Its Relation to Pathological Pain," convincing evidence has accumulated that indicates there are neuroplastic changes within the spinal cord in response to repeated exposure to opioids. Such neuroplastic changes occur at both cellular and intracellular levels. This is the point at which many people living with chronic pain enter the "chronic pain trance."

Unfortunately, most pain conditions in this country are treated with opiates; some research shows as high as 90 percent of people undergoing pain management are prescribed opiates at some point in their treatment. With so many people living with chronic pain and using opiates, the effects of neuroplastic changes need to be better understood.

I believe new healthy pathways or highways need to be developed for more effective pain management. My friend and colleague Terry Gorski uses the example of living in a rural area with an outhouse over a hundred yards from the back door. Between the back door and the outhouse is a field of heavy vegetation that is very hard to walk through.

On the first trip it takes a long time and is very difficult, but some of the vegetation gets tramped down just a little so the trip back is not quite as hard. After several trips it gets much easier.

I expand this metaphor by saying treatment is like gaining access to landscaping equipment that will assist you in putting in a paved path to your goal—effective pain management and an improved quality of life. Developing this "paved path" or new ways of thinking, more effective methods of managing painful emotions and new ways of behaving will improve your pain management and increase the quality of your life.

To complete this new path, new neuropathways need to be generated and used over and over until the highway is built. Unfortunately, people can be detoured, or lured, back to the old highways often because the old path is "known" and easy to navigate. One of the insidious consequences is that the farther a person travels down the "chronic pain trance" the less obvious it becomes.

Breaking the Chronic Pain Trance

So how do you break through a chronic pain trance? The first step is to realize you're in a trance to begin with which is often accompanied by different types of denial. You can learn to recognize and manage this denial by noticing what happens to your thinking and feelings when your denial gets challenged or triggered.

When denial is triggered stress levels go up, you get irritable, and can be easily angered. You may start to feel fearful, threatened, or unsure of yourself for no good reason. You may develop an inner conflict or start an argument in your head—for instance, one part of you wants to avoid looking at the problem. Another part of you, though, wants to take a good honest look at what is really going on, to set up a plan to move out of the problem and into a solution.

Identify and Manage Your Inner Saboteur—Also Known As...Denial

If you don't know whether or not you have a problem, it can be extremely difficult to find a solution.

Have you ever had an exciting dream or goal you wanted to accomplish, but denial got in your own way and sabotaged it? Sometimes we don't even realize how or why what we did set us up for failure. When you don't know you have a problem, it's difficult to accept there is any reason to find a solution. If we can't see it or we refuse to acknowledge self-defeating patterns that keep sabotaging us, we will never be able to overcome them.

There are different ways of talking about that part of ourselves that can protect or sabotage us—sometimes at the same time. Some people call this our *psychological defense system*, while others call it the *inner saboteur*. Have you ever heard the expression *the committee in your head* or *the angel or devil on your shoulder*? Many others think of the Zen concept called *monkey mind*. I will use the term denial.

Defining Denial

Following is a general explanation of denial that is used with permission from the *Denial Management Counseling Professional Guide*© by Terence T. Gorski and Stephen F. Grinstead:

> Denial is the natural tendency to avoid the pain that is caused by recognizing the presence, severity, and responsibility for dealing with serious problems... We all have a natural tendency to use denial to defend ourselves against the pain caused by overwhelming problems. Whenever we are forced to recognize a painful or overwhelming problem, our minds will activate a defensive program that protects us from the need to think or

talk about the problem. When we refuse to think or talk about the problem, the pain temporarily goes away. Unfortunately, so does our ability to recognize and deal effectively with the problem.

At times of high stress the brain can get emotionally overloaded. At these times the brain will activate automatic defenses, which I'm calling denial patterns. Each denial pattern is turned on by a specific trigger which threatens something that we value. When a severe problem causes intense stress, the brain activates intense fear and/or anger which in turn will activate an automatic psychological program. Automatic defensive thoughts and the urge to use resistant or self-defeating behaviors are mobilized.

This denial system is a major obstacle to recognizing self-sabotaging behaviors and achieving effective pain treatment. The psychological defense mechanism that protects us from devastating pain and problems is automatic and unconscious. It is important to remember that this defense system was developed to protect us from overwhelming pain and problems, or painful reality.

Whatever designation you use for this protective dynamic, it's really a combination of our mistaken thoughts, opinions, beliefs, and conclusions that have developed over our lifetime. Sometimes there is positive payoff; we feel protected while at the same time our needs get met. Unfortunately, this protection can also blind us and often hurts us more than helps.

I've worked with many people who were living with chronic pain and developed coexisting problems, including addiction, but were unaware it was happening. Some of them developed depression, anxiety, or sleep problems that they didn't manage well and experienced life damaging consequences as a result. Others had problems with their pain medication plan; they began abusing their prescription drugs, progressed into addiction and didn't even see it.

Denial Is a Normal and Natural Human Defense Mechanism

Just as the human body has an immune system to protect it from dangerous physical organisms, the human mind has a mental immune system to protect it from a painful reality. That mental immune system is our psychological defense system. The purpose of a psychological defense system is to protect our mind and personality.

Denial is one part of this defensive system. It is activated whenever we think or talk about a painful or overwhelming problem. There is nothing sick, pathological, or wrong about this. Denial is a normal and natural human response to painful reality.

There Are Four Levels of Denial

It is important to realize there are four levels of denial. The first level is simply a *lack of information.* In most cases, ineffective pain management or medication abuse/addiction is really just a lack of information. Having a belief that because a doctor prescribed pain medication, there won't be an addiction problem is an example of this first level. The solution is to provide a person with some up-to-date information about addiction. People living with chronic pain must learn as much as possible about their pain condition, effective pain management, and substance use problems that can result from taking prescription medications.

The second level of denial is *conscious defensiveness*. At this level a person knows that something is wrong, but they don't want to look closely and face the pain of knowing. The solution is to acknowledge the inner conflict where one part recognizes there's a problem, but another part doesn't want to admit it. To resolve this conflict we must be willing to listen to the part that knows the truth and take action. The old saying "the truth will set you free" is certainly relevant in this case.

The third level is *unconscious defensiveness*. A person at this level has stayed too long in their inner conflict and the defensive voice keeps winning. Once this happens, denial at this level becomes automatic and unconscious. The solution is much more difficult. It usually takes an outside intervention, or what is called a *motivational crisis*, to break through this defense and allow a person to know the truth so they can begin to address the problem. For some patients this motivational crisis was generated after their treating physicians became alarmed about their mismanaged chronic pain or increased use or abuse of pain medication. For others, family members intervened and urged them to seek help.

The fourth level is denial as a *delusional system*, which is the toughest to address. The delusion is a mistaken belief that is firmly held to be true despite convincing evidence that it is not. If someone was experiencing denial at this level, they probably wouldn't be open to reading this book. People at this level of denial usually need long-term psychotherapy and psychiatric medications to resolve their delusional system.

There Are Two Primary Antidotes for Denial: Acceptance and Problem Solving

Acceptance is a peaceful acknowledgement of the truth. If you can calmly face the problem, acknowledge the truth about what is going on, and accept that it is happening, you can then develop a way to handle the situation. The person who has accepted the truth of a serious problem has the ability to honestly affirm to themselves: "I have a serious problem! I am responsible for dealing with it! I'm willing to learn how!"

Problem solving is a system for finding solutions to your problems. Effective problem solving systems involve identification and clarification of your problems, identifying and projecting the logical consequences of alternatives, deciding which alternative to use, taking action, and evaluating the outcome. By recognizing and accepting the problem and developing an effective problem solving plan, your need to use denial will decrease because your ability to manage your problems will increase.

This was the reason I teamed up with Terence T. Gorski and Jennifer Messier to write the *Denial Management Counseling (DMC) for Effective Pain Management Workbook* that may also be a helpful resource for some of you reading this book. I believe that learning to identify and manage denial is a necessary first step for anyone living with chronic pain who wants to learn how to develop and implement an effective pain management plan.

The *DMC/Pain Workbook* is designed for people who have experienced significant problems related to living with chronic pain, but who honestly don't believe—or don't want to believe—that their decisions and behaviors are undermining what could be an effective pain management plan. It can be an important tool to help someone identify and manage their inner saboteur.

The Denial Pattern Checklist

Below are descriptions of twelve common denial patterns reprinted with permission from the *Denial Management Counseling (DMC) for Effective Pain Management Workbook.* As you read through the denial pattern checklist, check the ones you believe apply or have applied to you.

❑ 1.   **Avoidance:** Somewhere deep inside of me I'm afraid I might have a serious problem with how I am managing my pain. I don't want to think about it or talk about it. I'll do almost anything to avoid looking at what's going on with my pain management. Sometimes I become the master of distraction or find ways to throw people off track by not saying a word when they bring it up. Other times I act like I don't have

79

a clue what they are talking about when they mention concerns or I play "Uproar" and create a scene to lead them off track. They can't relate to me, they don't have my pain. I would rather isolate and deal with my pain by myself; I don't want to be a burden.

❑ 2. **Total Denial:** When others try to corner me, I tell the big lie. I don't have a problem with my pain management plan. No! Not me! Absolutely not! I am so good at convincing other people that there is nothing wrong with the way I am handling my pain sometimes I actually start believing it myself. When they believe my story a part of me feels really good because I beat them. Another small part of me feels disappointed. There is sometimes a small part that wants others to know what is really happening. That small scared part inside of me that wants help and is afraid that if I let people know how bad my pain or pain management plan is, they won't want to be around me or be in my life.

❑ 3. **Minimizing:** Sometimes things get so bad that I can't convince myself or others that I don't have a problem with my pain management plan and that I need to do something about it. When this happens I minimize. I make the problems with my pain management plan seem smaller than they really are. Yes, I had a small problem. But it only happened that once. It will never happen again. Besides, my pain management plan isn't as bad as people think it is. I don't have time to do all the work required to manage my pain more effectively. When my pain problems get worse, then I will do something about it.

❑ 4. **Rationalizing:** When there is no one around to blame, I use irrational thinking to create plausible explanations for my ineffective pain management. Sometimes I'll start *intellectualizing*. I'll try to explain my problems away. Sometimes I'll pretend to know a lot about pain management so I don't have to do the internal work that's really needed to effectively manage my pain. I'll quote articles that I read in the newspaper or heard on the news or saw on the Internet. I'll give the impression that I know so much about pain and pain management that advice from others is useless. The problem is, I never apply what I know about effective pain management to myself or open myself up to other peoples' recommendations.

❑ 5.   **Blaming:** When problems with my pain management plan get so bad that I can't deny or minimize them, I look for a scapegoat. I tell everyone that it's not my fault I have these problems with my pain management plan. It's somebody else's fault. I tell myself and others that I have done everything the doctors wanted and it's still not working. I only have these problems because of my partner/job/doctor. If you had pain problems like mine you wouldn't be able to do any better. If you had a doctor, job or a boss like mine, your pain condition would be unmanageable, too. I can't have a problem with my pain medications because the doctor prescribed them to me. So what if I have to take extra on some days, as long as I can blame someone else—anyone else—I can keep using the same self-defeating behaviors until that other person changes or they find the right answers for my pain. I don't have to be responsible for dealing with my pain more effectively; after all I'm not the expert!

❑ 6.   **Comparison:** I start to focus on other people's problems instead of my own. I work hard to convince myself that I don't need to do anything about my pain management plan right now because I can always find others that are worse off than me. Or, sometimes I compare myself to how easy life seems to be for those not suffering with my kind of pain condition. I focus on how easy other people have it and my depression gets worse. I tell myself that no one understands my pain and no one can help me because they don't know what it is like to be me and have my pain condition. I tell myself that unless others have "exactly" walked in my shoes, they can't help me with my pain management plan.

□ 7. **Compliance:** I start going through the motions of getting help for my problems with my pain management plan. I do what I'm told, no more and no less. I become compliant without honoring the fact I'm very skeptical or unmotivated to change. I promise to do things that I have no intention of doing just to get people off of my back and make it look like my pain management plan is getting better. I find excuses for not following through. When I get called on it, I tell people that I did the best that I could do and that what they've recommended is working as well as possible. I blame them for not giving me enough help. I tell people how sorry I am. I ask for another chance, make another half-hearted commitment, and the cycle of compliance starts all over again.

□ 8. **Manipulating:** When my problems start to box me into a corner, I start to manipulate and use the people who want to help me. I try to get them to handle all of my pain management issues and problems that have resulted because of my mismanaged pain. I get them to work harder on my pain problems than I am willing to, because I tell myself I don't have the energy or time to deal with this anymore. I'll let them help me, but only if they do it for me. I want a quick effortless fix. When they can't fix me, I blame them for my failure and use them as an excuse as to why I don't need to try anything new to help manage my pain. I won't let anyone make me do anything I don't want to do. If they try, I'll hurt myself, blame them, and try to make them feel guilty. There is a small part of me that enjoys the attention and energy people put into helping me manage my pain and I'm afraid of letting go of it.

❏ 9. **Having a Flight into Health:** I manage to put my pain management plan in action for a while and things start to get a little bit better. Instead of feeling motivated to do more, I convince myself that everything's fine now and I don't need to do anything else. I tell myself that I had a problem with my pain management, but I got a good pain program in place and it worked. I don't need to continue putting the energy and effort that I once did. I'm finally fine and I need to put my pain management problems behind me now and move on with my life.

❏ 10. **Fear of Change:** There is a big part of me that is ashamed to admit that I'm afraid to live life without my pain condition. I have become used to pain being my primary focus and identity, taking all my time and energy away from having to deal with other life responsibilities. I've become accustomed to other people focusing on my pain condition, as well as taking on most of the major responsibilities for my life. I'm afraid that if I get better I won't know how to take care of myself and my responsibilities that I've neglected because of my pain. I've gotten so used to everyone doing so much for me, that the thought of doing it all by myself is too overwhelming. Every time I find myself starting to make progress with my pain management, I get so afraid that I find myself sabotaging my progress. There is a part of me that feels a sense of relief every time I fail. Infrequently, there are times that I recognize another part of me who

83

doesn't want to continue living my life in this self-defeating way.

☐ 11. **Diagnosing Myself as Beyond Help:** I start to feel hopeless and that nothing will improve my pain condition. It seems like I've tried it *all* and nothing has worked. I don't believe that I can change how I manage my pain because all the doctors and experts I have gone to have failed me. There is a big part of me that just doesn't want to try anymore. It seems easier just to give up and stop trying. Sometimes I tell myself I would rather die than live like this one more day. When people try to help me, I brush them off by telling them that I'm hopeless and will never have an effective pain management plan. I dare people to try and help me. When they do I give them a hard time. They try to do my work for me and end up failing despite their best efforts. I don't understand why people keep trying to help me. It would be easier if they would let me keep going the way I have been. Can't they see how hopeless I really am and that no one will ever have a solution for me?

☐ 12. **I Have the Right to be This Way (Or, It's My Body):** I tell myself that this is my pain, my body, and I have a right to treat it any way I want. So what if the way I am managing my pain isn't working, or could even be harmful. I'll do anything to live without pain and no one has the right to tell me differently. I convince myself that I have a right to continue to use ineffective methods or do nothing even if it hurts me or those I love. Yes, I have a serious pain management problem. Yes, I'm destroying my life. Yes, I'm hurting those I love. Yes, I'm a burden to society. But so what! I have the right to do it my way. No one has the right to make me stop or tell me what I should be doing with my body.

Break Through the Chronic Pain Trance!

Recognition is only the first part of the solution for breaking through the self-defeating *chronic pain trance.* Years ago I was at a workshop presented by Dr. Stephen Covey, author of *The Seven Habits of Highly Effective People.* Dr. Covey made a statement that really hit me. "You can't think your way out of a problem you behaved your way into." In other words it's time to get into action.

Understanding and Coping with Irrational Thoughts and Uncomfortable Feelings on a Bad Pain Day

The information in this section was adapted from the *Addiction-Free Pain Management® Recovery Guide©* and is used with permission—the TFUAR (thinking, feelings, urges, actions, and reactions) process is part of the Gorski-CENAPS® Developmental Model for Recovery and Relapse Prevention. Below are some basic principles that will help you better understand how the TFUAR process works.

- **Thoughts cause feelings.** Whenever we think about something we automatically react by having a feeling or an emotion.

- **Thoughts and feelings work together to cause urges.** Your way of thinking causes you to feel certain feelings. These feelings, in turn, reinforce the way you are thinking. These thoughts and feelings work together to create an urge, or impulse, to do something. An urge is a desire that may be rational or irrational.

Sometimes the irrational urge is to isolate and give in to your depression. At other times you might be tempted to use inappropriate pain medication, including alcohol or other drugs, even though you know it will hurt you, which is also called *craving*. Other times you want to use self-defeating behaviors that at some level you know will not be good for you and could worsen your depression.

- **Urges plus decisions cause actions.** A decision is a choice. A choice is specific way of thinking that causes you to commit to one way of doing things while refusing to do anything else. The space between the urge and the action is always filled with a decision. This decision may be an automatic and unconscious choice that you have learned to make without having to think about it, or this decision can be based on a conscious choice that results from carefully reflecting on the situation and the options available for dealing with it.

- **Actions cause reactions from other people.** Your actions affect other people and cause them to react to you. It's helpful to think of your behavior as an invitation that you give to other people to treat you in certain ways. Some behaviors invite people to be nice to you and treat you with respect. Other behaviors invite people to argue and fight with you or put you down. In every social situation you share a part of the responsibility for what happens, because you are constantly inviting people to respond to you by the actions you take and how you react to what other people do. Sometimes these reactions help you manage your pain more effectively, but at other times lead to increased stress levels that cause you to make poor decisions.

When you experience serious depression or higher levels of pain your TFUARs often change. The purpose of the following exercise is to explore your personal accounts in each of the above TFUAR areas when you experience pain on a bad, or high pain level, day.

Moving from the Problem into the Solution

When you experience negative consequences as a result

of completing the TFUAR process, you will usually have one or more of the following problems:

- You can't tell the difference between thoughts and feelings. You tend to believe that you can think anything you want and it won't affect your feelings. When you start to have uncomfortable feelings you can't understand why and convince yourself that the only way to feel better is to use self-defeating behaviors that worked for you in the past, including inappropriate pain medication, alcohol or other drugs.
- You can't tell the difference between feelings and urges. You believe that each feeling carries with it a specific urge. You don't understand that you can experience a feeling and not do anything about it. You don't realize that you can sit still, breathe into the feeling, and watch it go away without acting out on it.
- You can't tell the difference between urges and actions. You don't realize there is a space between an urge and action called the decision point.
- You can't control your impulses. You believe you must do whatever you feel an urge to do. You have never learned how to control your impulses. You were never taught how to pause, relax, reflect, and make a decision when feeling a strong urge to act immediately. Let's look at the four steps to managing impulse control:
  1. *Pause* and notice the urge without doing anything about it;
  2. *Relax* by taking a deep breath in, slowly exhale and consciously imagine the stress draining from your body;
  3. *Reflect* on what you are experiencing by asking yourself: "What do I have an urge to do? What has happened when I have done similar things in the past? What is likely to happen if I do that now?"
  4. *Decide* what you are going to do about the urge. Make

a conscious choice instead of acting out in an automatic and unconscious way. When making a choice about what you are going to do, remind yourself that you will be responsible for both the action that you choose to take and its consequence.

Remember: *Impulse control lives in the space between the urge and the action.*

• You can't tell the difference between actions and social reactions. You tend to believe that people respond to you for no reason at all. You don't link the responses of others to what you do when you are with them. In reality how we behave is an invitation to other people to treat us in certain ways. Ask yourself: "How do I want to behave in this situation so that other people will treat me the way I want to be treated?"

Learning how to identify and rate the intensity of your emotions is crucial.

As you'll see in the following chapter, understanding and addressing the emotional components of chronic pain is very important. Below you will see a simple feeling/emotional checklist that was developed by Terence T. Gorski and the CENAPS® Corporation. Use this checklist to describe how you tend to feel when you're experiencing depression and/or chronic pain at its worst (or on a bad day), and how intense each feeling is on a scale of 1 (lowest intensity) to 10 (highest intensity). Please realize that you may feel neither of the two choices with each pair. Just identify and rate the ones that apply to you. Do you tend to feel on a bad pain day...?

☐ Strong   or   ☐ Weak
                             How strong is the feeling (0–10)? _____

☐ Safe   or   ☐ Threatened
                             How strong is the feeling (0–10)? _____

☐ Angry	or	☐ Caring
☐ Fulfilled	or	☐ Frustrated
☐ Happy	or	☐ Sad
☐ Connected	or	☐ Lonely
☐ Proud	or	☐ Ashamed, Guilty
☐ Peaceful	or	☐ Agitated

☐ Angry or ☐ Caring
How strong is the feeling (0–10)? _____

☐ Fulfilled or ☐ Frustrated
How strong is the feeling (0–10)? _____

☐ Happy or ☐ Sad
How strong is the feeling (0–10)? _____

☐ Connected or ☐ Lonely
How strong is the feeling (0–10)? _____

☐ Proud or ☐ Ashamed, Guilty
How strong is the feeling (0–10)? _____

☐ Peaceful or ☐ Agitated
How strong is the feeling (0–10)? _____

Mary's and Mark's TFUAR Insights

Mark identified his three irrational thinking patterns: (1) Why is this happening to me; (2) I have to do whatever it takes to stop this; and (3) This sucks, life isn't worth living. Mark tends to react using a combination of thinking patterns: he vacillates between a *top-dog/*power position, and an *underdog/*victim position. Mary, on the other hand, had a strong tendency to stay in the *underdog/*victim position as evidenced by her thinking statements: (1) Nobody cares about me; (2) God is punishing me; and (3) I'll never get better—this will never end.

Both Mary and Mark identified similar feelings: weak, angry, sad, lonely, threatened, and frustrated. Mary rated weak at level 10 while Mark rated it level 5. Mary rated sad at level 8 and Mark rated it 4. Mary rated threatened at level 9 while Mark was at level 10. Both rated anger and frustration at level 10. Mary rated ashamed at level 10 while Mark rated it level *20,* even though this was only a 10-point scale. In addition, Mark rated agitated at level 10, stating; "I'm never comfortable in my own skin and I want to lash out." Mark did often "lash out" at others, but mostly he indulged in self-destructive behaviors that only hurt him.

Mary identified a negative self-defeating urge: "I want to stay in bed and pull the covers up." Mark identified "I'll just pop a couple of extra pills." Both Mary and Mark also had an urge to commit suicide. Mark often used pain medication and if none was available he would find other self-defeating ways to distract himself. Mary tended to cry or try to sleep to escape.

Both Mary and Mark tended to isolate, with Mark hiding his pain using a tough façade. Mary felt too much shame and guilt to reach out, even to her church friends, and then felt guilty and ashamed about that. The result for both of them was isolation from their support networks, which is a common behavior for people experiencing chronic pain. Mary also identified the following social reactions: "I'm always yelling at my family so they avoid being around me." When Mark wasn't putting on the tough guy façade he also identified "I isolate and people give up on me."

Developing Your TFUAR Management Plan

Please take a brief timeout to breathe and center yourself. When you are ready, complete the following exercise, which is designed to help you identify, challenge, and change your thoughts, manage your feelings, urges, actions, and social reactions that can lead to using self-defeating behaviors. These defeating behaviors often result in negative consequences that lead to a worsening of your depression and/or chronic pain symptoms.

Please Stop and Take Time to Read the Following Directions Then Complete Your TFUAR Exercise in the Following Section

Thinking: First, draw a line down the middle of a page so you have two columns. Title the left-hand column PROBLEM and the right-hand column SOLUTION. Thinking of your pain on a bad pain day, please list three self-defeating or negative thoughts that you experienced. Now in the right-hand column come up with as many positive challenges or affirmations that you can to challenge those self-defeating thoughts.

Feelings: Again draw a line down the middle of a page so you have two columns—if you have room under the thinking section just continue from there. Title the left-hand column PROBLEM and the right-hand column SOLUTION. Thinking of your pain on a bad pain day and the self-defeating thoughts you listed above, please list three uncomfortable feelings or emotions that you experience as a result of those thoughts and rate them on a 1–10 scale. In the solution column come up with as many positive ways you can think of to manage your feelings that would help you in this situation.

Urges: Continue the line down the middle of a page so you keep two columns. Again the left-hand column is the PROBLEM and the right-hand column is the SOLUTION. Thinking of your pain on a bad pain day with your self-defeating thoughts and uncomfortable emotions, please list three self-defeating or negative urges or impulses that you want to do. In the right-hand column come up with as many positive ways that you can think of that will challenge those self-defeating urges.

Actions: Continue the line down the middle of a page

so you keep two columns. Again the left-hand column is the PROBLEM and the right-hand column is the SOLUTION. Thinking of your pain on a bad pain day with your self-defeating thoughts, uncomfortable emotions and self-defeating urges, list three self-destructive or negative actions or behaviors you use. In the right-hand column come up with as many positive actions that you can think of that will challenge those self-destructive actions or behaviors. What are your new healthy behaviors that you can implement?

Reactions: Continue the line down the middle of a page so you keep two columns. Again, the left-hand column is the PROBLEM and the right-hand column is the SOLUTION. Finally, thinking of your pain on a bad pain day with your self-defeating thoughts, uncomfortable emotions, self-defeating urges, and self-destructive actions, please list three ways your behavior causes negative reactions from the people around you. In the right-hand column list as many guides, helpers or coaches as you can to support you. Then list all the ways you can think of for these healthy support people to say or do things that will aid you.

Your finished exercise should look something like the chart on page 93, but with your personal TFUARs filled in on both the problem and solution sides.

This helps you break the chronic pain trance.

Nature abhors a vacuum so it's important that you replace unhealthy defense mechanisms with new alternatives or your old patterns of behavior will resurface. Part of the solution is educating yourself. Knowledge is power. The re-

Problem	Solution
Thinking	Thinking
Feelings	Feelings
Urges	Urges
Actions	Actions
Reactions	Reactions

mainder of this book is designed to increase your understanding of pain so you can take action, stop suffering, and break the chronic pain trance.

You're now on the journey. As you complete your first call to action step, please take some time to review your first step. Look over Mary's and Mark's stories and actions they have taken, and then think about the insights you have gained so far.

Your First Step Call to Action

You have now completed the first step of your pain management journey and here is your opportunity to summarize your experience so far. Please answer the three questions below:

1. What is the most important thing you have learned about yourself and your pain management as a result of completing this step?

_____

_____

_____

_____

_____

_____

2. What are you willing to commit to do differently as a result of what you have learned by completing this step?

_____

_____

_____

_____

_____

_____

3. What obstacles might get in the way of your making these changes and what can you do to overcome those roadblocks? _____

_____

_____

_____

_____

_____

_____

**Please Take Time to Pause,
Rest, and Reflect
Then Go on to Step Two**

Step Two:
Taking a Fresh Look at Your Relationship with Pain

Below are some excerpts from "Pain: Moving from Symptom Control toward Mechanism-Specific Pharmacologic Management," a review written by Clifford J. Woolf, MD; for *Physiology in Medicine: A Series of Articles Linking Medicine with Science* (2004), 140:6, 441–451. Dr. Woolf discusses pain from a more technical perspective than you will see later. I'll use his information as a starting point to introduce you to a fuller understanding of pain than you may have learned before.

Pain is a multidimensional sensory experience that is intrinsically unpleasant and associated with hurting and soreness. It may vary in intensity (mild, moderate, or severe), quality (sharp, burning, or dull), duration (transient, intermittent, or persistent), and referral (superficial or deep, localized or diffuse). Although it is essentially a sensation, pain has strong cognitive and emotional components. It is also associated with avoidance motor reflexes and alterations in autonomic output. All of these traits are inextricably linked in the experience of pain.

Pain can be essentially divided into two broad categories: adaptive and maladaptive. Adaptive pain contributes to survival by protecting the organism from injury or promoting healing when injury has occurred. Maladaptive pain, in contrast, is an expression of the pathologic operation of the nervous system; it is pain as disease.

The sensory experience of acute pain caused by a noxious stimulus is mediated by a specialized high-threshold sensory system, the nociceptive system. This system extends from the periphery through the spinal cord, brain stem, and thalamus to the cerebral cortex, where the sensation is perceived. To prevent damage to tissue, we have learned to associate certain categories of stimuli with danger that must be avoided if at all possible. This association is formed by linking noxious stimuli with a sensation that is intense and unpleasant: that is, pain. The sensation of pain must be strong enough that it demands immediate attention.

Defining Pain

There are a number of definitions for pain. The most widely accepted one is used by the International Association for the Study of Pain. It defines pain as, "An unpleasant sensory and emotional experience arising from actual or potential tissue damage or described in terms of such damage."

On the Internet, the *Encyclopedia Britannica* defines pain as, "A complex experience consisting of a physiological (bodily) response to a noxious stimulus followed by an affective (emotional) response to that event. Pain is a warning mechanism that helps to protect an organism by influencing it to withdraw from harmful stimuli. It is primarily associated with injury or the threat of injury to bodily tissues."

The American Academy of Pain Medicine (AAPM) defines pain as, "An unpleasant sensation and emotional response to that sensation."

The definition of pain that some believe is the most appropriate for use in clinical practice was put forth by Margo McCaffery in 1968. She defined pain as "whatever the experiencing person says it is, existing whenever and wherever the person says it does."

Pain Is a Signal that Communicates Information

The easiest way to understand pain is to recognize that every time you feel pain, your body is attempting to tell you that something is wrong. Pain sensations are critical to human survival. Without pain you would have no way of knowing that something is wrong with your body. So without pain you would be unable to take action to correct the problem or situation that is causing your pain.

What Is Your Pain Trying to Tell You?

As I stated in the first chapter, whenever you are experiencing pain, it's always helpful to ask: "What is my pain trying to tell me?" Remember, the function of pain is to tell us that something is wrong, that we better find out what it is and find a way to fix it.

To understand the language of pain, you must learn to understand how pain echoes and reverberates between the physical, psychological, and social dimensions of the human condition. Pain is truly a total human experience that affects all aspects of human functioning.

When it comes to managing your pain, knowledge is power. Once you know what is really going on with your body and mind, you can take action to effectively manage it. In fact, you must embrace pain as your friend and stop believing it's your enemy. This is easier said than done and many of my patients have looked at me like I'm crazy when I tell them they must make peace with their pain. They often tell me it's hard to accept, but nevertheless it's true.

Stop believing pain is your enemy!
Make peace with your pain!
Start embracing pain as your friend!

Not only have I been working as a therapist and trainer in the field of chronic pain and coexisting problems for more than three decades, I have also been living with my own chronic pain condition during that time. I still have periodic episodes of pain flare-ups where I need to put into practice all that I've learned. Like everyone living with a chronic pain

97

condition some days are better than others, but even on the bad days, one thing is certain—*pain does not control my life.*

Making peace with my pain was something I had to resolve for myself early on in my own chronic pain management journey. I always ask the patients I work with and the clinicians I train to consider this question—*are you willing to make peace with your pain or do you want to continue to suffer?* In essence what I'm asking them is: "Are you willing to do what is necessary to make pain your friend and move on with your life?" As you can imagine and maybe you're thinking this yourself, they believe I've lost my mind and have told me so in no uncertain terms! Nevertheless, the question opened the door for a deeper level of healing to begin.

When you are willing to consider that you can make pain an ally instead of an enemy, the next step is to develop an effective chronic pain management plan. This starts with learning all you can about your pain and how to intervene in an appropriate way that continually improves the quality of your life.

Our pain system is a crucial component of the human body and essential to our survival. Can you imagine what would happen if we didn't have pain receptors and we kept putting ourselves in situations that seriously damaged our body? Picture this: you're in the kitchen talking on the phone and you inadvertently put your hand down on a hot stove burner. Without pain receptors your first indication that something was wrong would be the smell of burning flesh—yours!

As I mentioned above, it can be helpful to ask: "What is my pain trying to tell me?" Sometimes though, it can be difficult, if not impossible, to pinpoint the pain generator. So, we can get frustrated because as human beings we want to know why something is happening.

When we're experiencing pain, the more important question is, "What can I do, right now to manage my pain in a healthy way that supports me physically, emotionally, and spiritually?" The answer will be different for each person. But what if you don't know the answer because your pain has become unmanageable, no matter what you try? This brings us to a discussion of *pain versus suffering* which I will cover in the next chapter.

Understanding the Pain System

Every human being has a pain system that is a combination of pain receptors and pain circuits. You also have specialized and general pain receptors and circuits. These receptors and circuits usually function very well, alerting you when something is wrong.

- Pain receptors are nerve cells that detect when something is wrong.
- Pain circuits are a series of nerve cells that transmit the message to your brain that something is wrong.
- Pain is the signal or warning that indicates something is wrong.

Physically, the experience of pain originates in receptors that are located throughout the body. Some of these receptors are located deep within the body, providing sensations about muscle aches, pulled tendons, and fluid-filled, swollen joints. Other receptors, such as in the skin, provide pain sensations when cuts, burns or abrasions have occurred near the surface of the body. Many times the skin receptors respond to the signal generated from the localized damage to tissue. For example, a skin cut will essentially cause various cells to produce and release a variety of chemical messengers that stimulate pain receptors into action from the area of injury.

The Gate Control Theory of Pain

The *gate control theory of pain* was developed originally

by Melzack and Wall in the early 1960s. It changed the way pain perception was viewed. The basis of this theory is that physical pain is not a direct result of the activation of pain receptor neurons, but rather the perception of pain is modulated by the interaction between different neurons. This theory also proposes that cognitive and emotional factors influence the perception of pain—there are more than just physiological factors involved.

How This Theory of Chronic Pain Works

Your brain commonly blocks out sensations that it knows are not dangerous, such as the discomfort of tight-fitting shoes that are put on in the morning, then feeling OK just a short time later. A similar process is at work in processing some moderately painful experiences.

In the gate control theory, the experience of pain depends on a complex interplay of two systems as they each process pain signals in their own way. Upon injury, pain messages originate in nerves associated with the damaged tissue and flow along the peripheral nerves to the spinal cord and on up to the brain.

The gate control theory asserts that before pain messages can reach the brain, they encounter *nerve gates* in the spinal cord that open or close depending on a number of factors (including instructions coming down from the brain). When the gates are open, pain messages *get through* more or less easily and pain can be intense. When the gates close, pain messages are prevented from reaching the brain and pain may not even be experienced. The gate control theory attempts to explain the experience of pain (including psychological factors) on a physiological level.

Deardorff (2004) states that when living with chronic pain it is important to understand the gate control theory, as this explains what factors can open and close the spinal nerve gates. An in-depth exploration of the gate control theory is beyond the scope of this book, but you can refer to the books mentioned in the Appendix under Melzack and Wall (1965 & 1982) and Deardorff (1997 & 2004).

Acute versus Chronic Pain

It's also important to understand the difference between acute pain and chronic pain, especially when there is a need to manage pain with potentially addictive medication. Acute pain tells your body that something is wrong or that damage to the system has occurred. The source of the pain is often easily identified, and typically does not last very long. An example of acute pain is when you touch a hot burner on the stove.

Acute pain is short-lived, chronic pain lasts much longer.

A chronic pain condition will linger long after the initial injury, sometimes for years. In many cases chronic pain no longer serves a useful purpose. To be considered a chronic pain condition, some people say the symptoms must continue for at least six months, while others look at 30 days as the typical transition time. Some examples of chronic pain are back pain, fibromyalgia, or frequent cluster headaches.

Bio-Psycho-Social Components of Pain

In order to understand pain management you need to first recognize that pain is a total biopsychosocial experience that is made up of three components—biological, psychological, and social/cultural.

Pain is a biopsychosocial experience.

When you're in pain, you hurt physically. You psychologically respond to the pain by thinking, feeling, and acting. You think about the pain and try to figure out what is causing it and why you're hurting. You experience emotional reactions to the pain. You may get angry, frightened, or frustrated by your pain. You talk about your pain with family, friends, and coworkers who help you develop a social and cultural context for assigning meaning to your personal pain experience and decide what action to take.

Neuropathic Chronic Pain

If you are living with neuropathic pain like I am, you know treatment can be frustrating and often ineffective. While acute short-term pain is usually easy to manage, and many chronic pain conditions can be treated effectively, treating neuropathic pain can be a big challenge for both the person with pain and their healthcare providers.

When you have neuropathic pain, the peripheral or central nervous systems are malfunctioning and become the cause of the pain. It is usually perceived as a steady burning, "pins and needles," or "electric shock" sensation and/or tickling. The difference is due to the fact that "ordinary" pain stimulates only pain nerves, while a neuropathy often results in the firing of both pain and non-pain (touch, warm, cool) sensory nerves in the same area, producing signals that the spinal cord and brain do not normally expect to receive.

Neuropathic pain is produced by damage to, or pathological changes in the peripheral or central nervous systems. This type of pain is often a result of pain signals getting turned on, but not getting turned off. Unfortunately, neuropathic pain often responds poorly to standard pain treatments; occasionally the pain symptoms may get worse instead of better over time. For some people, this can lead to serious disability and a significantly decreased quality of life.

This is why early recognition and aggressive management of this type of pain is so important for successful treatment outcomes. What is most helpful are the different types of treatments provided by a multidisciplinary pain management team.

There are many differences of opinion on the "right" type of medication management approaches for treating neuropathic pain conditions. Some healthcare providers think opiates are a good first line treatment approach, while others think they are not appropriate. If you are experiencing neuropathic pain, learn as much as you can about it and discuss all the treatment options with your healthcare provider.

Chronic Pain and the Hijacked Brain

I want to emphasize again, that in order to achieve the best quality of life and level of functioning, you must educate yourself about the subject of pain and what constitutes effective pain management. The next few sections will continue that education. We know that pain is a signal that tells us there is damage or something wrong with our system.

However, with some chronic pain conditions the system (including the brain) gets altered. The pain system gets turned on and cannot be turned off. I call this the "hijacked" brain. It is also called neuroplasticity which I talked about in step one. Again, it refers to changes that occur in the organization of the brain as a result of experience. I'll talk more about neuroplasticity in step three. With neuroplasticity, brain activity that is associated with a given function can move to a different location as a consequence of normal experience or brain damage/recovery. In the case of chronic pain this can mean that pain signals keep occurring despite lack of a trigger or tissue damage.

According to research published in *Annals of the New York Academy of Sciences* 933:175–184 (2001) titled "Spinal Cord Neuroplasticity following Repeated Opioid Exposure and Its Relation to Pathological Pain," convincing evidence has accumulated that indicates there are neuroplastic changes within the spinal cord in response to repeated exposure to opioids.

Such neuroplastic changes occur at both cellular and intracellular levels. Unfortunately, most pain conditions in this country are treated with opiates—some research shows as high as 90 percent of people undergoing pain management are prescribed opiates at some point in their treatment process. With so many people living with chronic pain and using opiates, these neuroplastic changes need to be better understood.

I like to use simple language and metaphors or visual images when educating my patients. Many people may not understand the term *neuroplasticity* so I use the metaphor of the hijacked brain.

I tell them the reality of neuroplastic science is much more complex, but in essence what happens is that the brain forms pathways (called neuronetworks) that eventually become superhighways—in other words the new neuronetwork becomes more complex and elaborate.

To reduce or eliminate pain, a number of factors are involved, but an important one is to replace old pain behaviors that produce suffering. In order to do this, new brain pathways need to be developed.

It is crucial to develop new ways of thinking, more effective methods of managing painful emotions, and new ways of behaving that will improve your pain management and quality of life.

To accomplish these improvements, new neuropathways need to be generated and used over and over until the highway is built. Unfortunately, there are obstacles that can get in the way that detour people back to their old neuro-highways.

The Addiction-Free Pain Management® (APM) System is designed to assist people in building these new brain pathways to address obstacles to effective pain management. One of the most common obstacles is a pain flare-up caused by painful or stressful situations.

Three Essential Levels of Pain Management

Modern pain management systematically approaches the treatment of pain at all three levels (bio-psycho-social) simultaneously. This means using physical treatments to reduce the intensity of your physical pain. It also means using psychological treatments to identify and change your thoughts, feelings, and behaviors that are making your pain more intense and replacing them with positive thinking, as well as feeling and behavior management skills that can reduce the intensity of your pain. Finally, effective pain management must involve not only you, but also the significant people in your life who can help you develop a social and cultural context in which to experience your pain in a way that will reduce suffering.

Biological pain is a signal that something is going wrong with your body. The biological, or physical, pain sensations are critical to human survival. Without pain we would have no way of knowing that something was wrong with our body. So, without pain we would be unable to take action to correct the problem or deal with the situation that is causing our pain.

Psychological pain results from the meaning you assign to the pain signal. The psychological symptoms include both cognitive (thinking changes) and emotional (uncomfortable feelings) that lead to suffering. Most people are not able to differentiate between the physical and psychological. All they know is "I hurt and I want relief."

Social and cultural pain, results from the social and cultural meaning assigned by other people to the pain you are experiencing, and whether or not the pain is recognized as being severe enough to warrant a socially approved *sick* role. These three components determine whether the signal from your body to your brain is interpreted as pain or suffering.

Imagine the following vignette: Bob is a star football player at his college. In last week's homecoming game Bob scored the winning touchdown, but broke his arm in the process. This week Bob is sitting on the bench with a cast on his arm that everyone has signed. This cast and how he *earned* it are seen as an honorable reason for him to be sitting on the bench.

In that same game Karl, a big hulking lineman, "tweaked" his back and was also sitting on the bench this week. Unlike Bob, Karl doesn't have an observable injury and people were asking him why he wasn't out on the field helping his team. Karl is much more likely than Bob to experience shame or guilt, which will probably amplify his pain symptoms.

The Spiritual Aspects of Chronic Pain Management

Chronic pain is often misunderstood and undertreated. One reason may be that in addition to the biopsychosocial impact of chronic pain, a spiritual crisis frequently accompanies the condition. This is a body-mind-spirit problem that needs a multifaceted solution including addressing the spiritual component of pain. Spiritual healing can be an effective complementary and alternative approach.

Many people have found spiritual interventions like the traditions of prayer and meditation to contribute to the easing of their suffering. Unfortunately, in our fast-paced world and our secular treatment modality, the spiritual component of chronic pain management does not receive enough attention.

Another problem is that many people confuse religion with spirituality. Although the terms *religion* and *spirituality* are sometimes used interchangeably, they are really separate concepts. Religion is an organized faith system grounded in institutional standards, practices, and core beliefs. On the other hand, spirituality is grounded in personal beliefs and practices that can be experienced with or without a formal religion.

So what is spirituality? Let's look at some different definitions.

> **Merriam-Webster Online Dictionary states:** 1. something that in ecclesiastical law belongs to the church or to a cleric as such; 2. clergy; 3. sensitivity or attachment to religious values; 4. the quality or state of being spiritual.
>
> **YourDictionary.com states:** 1. spiritual character, quality, or nature; 2. religious devotion or piety; 3. the rights, jurisdiction, tithes, etc. belonging to the church or to an ecclesiastic; 4. the fact or state of being incorporeal.
>
> **The online *Wikipedia* encyclopedia defines spirituality as:** Spirituality is relating to, consisting of, or having the nature of spirit; not tangible or material. Synonyms include immaterialism, dualism, incorporeality and eternity. Spirituality is associated with religion, deities, the supernatural, and an afterlife, although the decline of organized religion in the West and the growth of secularism has brought about a wider understanding of its nature.

Spirituality versus Religion

Over the years I have found it important to have a discussion with my patients regarding how spirituality applies to effective pain management, and to develop a common understanding of the terms we will use in our work together. One concept that rings true for a number of my patients is a simple saying: "Religion prepares people for the next life while spirituality helps them live this life to their full potential." Many of my colleagues recommend clarifying the difference between the terms "spirituality" and "religion." They advocate developing a broad-based definition of spirituality that encompasses religious and nonreligious perspectives.

Spirituality is a complex and multidimensional part of the human experience. It involves beliefs, perceptions, thoughts, feelings, experiences, and behavioral aspects. Thoughts, beliefs, and perceptions include the search for meaning, purpose, and truth in life and the values by which a person lives their life. The experiential and emotional aspects involve feelings of hope, love, connection, inner peace, comfort, and support. The behavioral aspects of spirituality involve the way a person externally demonstrates their individual spiritual beliefs and inner spiritual state.

I've know many people who are very religious, but lack true spirituality and have met many others who demonstrate powerful spiritual principles who were not part of any organized religion. However, many people do find spirituality through religion or through a personal relationship with the divine, while others find it through a connection to nature, through music and the arts, through a set of values and principles or through a quest for scientific truth.

Pain versus Suffering

Chronic pain is often associated with perceived endless, meaningless suffering. Given the definition that spirituality is a basic human phenomenon that allows the creation of meaning and purpose in life, a person's spiritual beliefs can influence their health and sense of well-being. Spiritual issues related to the suffering of chronic pain involve an interaction between emotions such as fear, guilt, anger, loss, and despair. Often this suffering seems inseparable from the physical pain a person experiences and can influence the way they express their pain.

The psychological meaning that people assign to a physical pain signal will determine whether they simply feel pain ("Ouch, this hurts!") or experience suffering ("Because I hurt, something awful or terrible is happening!"). Although pain and suffering are often used interchangeably, there is an important distinction that needs to be made. Pain is an unpleasant signal (sometimes very unpleasant) telling people that something is wrong with their body. Suffering results from the meaning or interpretation the brain assigns to the pain signal. You will learn much more about pain versus suffering in the next chapter.

The concept of healing spiritual pain requires that you to go beyond the bounds of traditional clinical treatments and be prepared to devote the time required to develop supportive and understanding relationships with people who care. It is crucial to add the spiritual aspects of pain in a multi-dimensional treatment plan.

It's difficult to fully understand or measure spirituality using the scientific method, yet convincing evidence in the medical literature supports its beneficial role in the practice of medicine. It will take many more years of study to understand exactly which aspects of spirituality hold the most benefit for health and well-being. The world's great wisdom traditions suggest that some of the most important aspects of spirituality lie in the sense of connection and inner strength, comfort, love, and peace that individuals derive from their relationship with self, others, nature, and the transcendent.

I believe that for many people spiritual healing can be an important component of a multifaceted treatment plan. One goal of spiritual healing is to improve your well-being and quality of life, rather than to cure specific diseases or in this case eliminate pain. Components of spiritual healing may include visualization, prayer, meditation, and positive thinking.

Since chronic pain impacts your body, mind, and spirit, the solution must address all of these areas. This takes a multidisciplinary approach that greatly benefits by including a spiritual healing practitioner on your team. The ultimate goal of effective chronic pain management is to increase your quality of life on all levels.

Looking at the Whole Person

It is also important to take a look at all areas of the self:

(1) the physical self; (2) the psychological (thinking and feeling) self; (3) the social/cultural aspects of self; and (4) the spiritual aspects of self. These are also the four areas that are impacted when living with chronic pain on a daily basis. If the treatment plan does not adequately address all four areas, chronic pain management will not be as effective—or it may lead to ongoing suffering.

Many times in the Western medicine approach one area is not addressed at all—the spiritual. I see the spiritual aspect of self as the glue that contains and nourishes all three of the other areas and always ask my patients to explore this important part. Please see the diagram below.

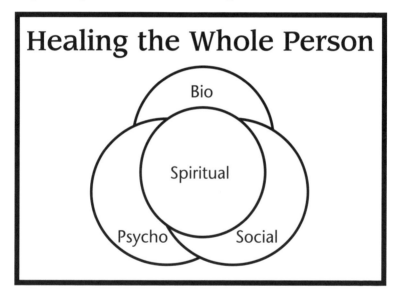

Healing the Whole Person

Bio

Spiritual

Psycho   Social

I believe healing must address the whole person in order to obtain the best treatment outcomes and an effective chronic pain management plan—not to mention freedom from suffering. Part of my initial evaluation session with my patients includes scoring each of the four areas of self—bio-psycho-social-spiritual. Each area is scored on a 1- to 25-point scale and that score is your starting point—if it's low, don't worry we can bring it up, and if it seems high, don't get complacent because it can always come down.

I also explain some of the important components needed in each of the four areas before I ask them to give me their score. In the biological area I cover interventions such as diet and nutrition; sleep hygiene; activity pacing; stress management; eliminating or reducing nicotine, caffeine, and sugar; as well as having an effective medication management plan in place. Then I explain the scoring; if the score is one to three you should probably be hospitalized in the intensive care unit. If you score 25, you're ready to run a triathlon.

In the psychological area I list examples like managing self-defeating defense mechanisms (also know as *denial*), positive thinking and feeling management plans, therapy or counseling, and daily balanced structure. Here I explain that if this score is one to three, they need to be in the hospital, but this time in the psychiatric ward. If their score is 25, they've reached enlightenment or guru status.

Next is the social area where I list ideas such as letting go of enabling friends and family members, setting assertive limits and boundaries, developing a chronic pain support system, and connecting and communicating with family and friends in a healthy manner. This time if the score is one to three they are hermits ready for a cave, and if it's 25 they are a well-connected social butterfly.

Finally, the spiritual area is where I list ideas such as prayer, meditation, finding peace in nature, working the steps if in a Twelve-Step program, spiritual practice, and religious practice. This time if the score is one to three, they are totally cut off from their spiritual connection, and if it's 25 they are in total harmony.

Then I have them pick a goal in their lowest scored area and commit to a proactive plan of action that will raise that score. When that's accomplished, I have them go to the next lowest box and do the same thing. Then they complete that process for the final two areas. I explain the goal is to keep moving forward. This healing process is like walking up a down escalator; if you stop you go down.

People who are willing to develop a treatment plan that includes medication management, psychological/emotional healing, social/cultural and spiritual growth have a much better chance of obtaining effective chronic pain management and freedom from suffering. Remember that although this is a right, it is also a responsibility.

Anxiety, Trauma, and Sleep Problems

In the next three sections you'll see how anxiety, trauma, and sleep problems need to be understood and managed in order for you to become free from suffering. These three components also contribute to how you perceive and handle your personal relationship with chronic pain.

The Role of Anxiety in Chronic Pain Management

In most cases, anxiety about pain is more likely in the acute pain stage, while depression prevails in the ongoing chronic pain stage. A subacute stage occurs after the acute stage, but before the chronic stage and usually occurs within the three- to six-month range.

At the acute stage the person in pain generally feels a reasonable sense of hope that the pain will resolve within the near future. In the subacute stage and at the beginning of the chronic stage, people's thoughts and emotions about the pain begin to change.

At this point it isn't uncommon for the person to begin to wonder if the pain will ever go away or if they'll ever get better. These types of thoughts lead to anxiety. Although most people believe that their anxiety will subside *when the pain goes away*, the anxiety frequently leads to a significant increase in pain perception, which results in a vicious cycle of pain, anxiety, more pain, and more anxiety.

Anxiety can occur at different intensities, all the way from mild nervousness to full-blown panic attacks. Anxiety can be characterized by the following:

- Muscle tension, including shaking, jitters, trembling, muscle aches, fatigue, restlessness, and inability to relax.
- Nervous system hyperactivity, including sweaty palms, racing heart, dry mouth, upset stomach, diarrhea, lump in throat, and shortness of breath.
- Apprehensive expectations, including anxiety, worry, fear, anticipation of misfortune.
- Trouble concentrating, including distractibility, insomnia, feelings of edginess or irritability, and impatience.

Excess anxiety and tension can cause you to experience heightened emotional upset (such as, anxiety, depression, and anger), increased pain, slower healing times, and increased side effects related to medication, among other things. An ongoing stress response causes numerous negative problems such as increasing muscle tension and pain, while also decreasing the activity of your immune system and blood flow to your extremities.

Common Chronic Pain Conditions and Diseases that Occur with Anxiety Conditions

According to the Anxiety Disorders Association of America (ADAA), chronic pain conditions are highly prevalent in people with anxiety disorders. The following are among the most common reported by the ADAA:

Arthritis—Arthritis is a wide-ranging term that describes a group of more than 100 medical conditions that affect the musculoskeletal system and specifically the joints, which are where two or more bones meet. Arthritis-related joint problems include pain, stiffness, inflammation, and damage to joint cartilage and surrounding structures. Damage can lead to joint weakness, instability, and deformities that may interfere with even the most basic daily tasks. Some forms of arthritis are systemic, meaning they can affect the whole body and can cause damage to virtually any bodily organ or system.

The prevalence of anxiety and mood disorders (such as depression) is higher in individuals with arthritis than in the general population. Some studies have found anxiety disorders are even more strongly associated with arthritis than is depression. A co-occurring anxiety disorder or mood disorder is more often found in arthritis sufferers in younger age groups.

Fibromyalgia—Fibromyalgia is characterized by widespread musculoskeletal aches, pain, and stiffness, soft-tissue tenderness, general fatigue, and sleep problems. The most common areas of pain include the neck, back, shoulders, pelvic girdle, and hands, but any part of the body can be affected. People with fibromyalgia experience a range of symptoms that can vary in intensity. Symptoms may also include irritable bowel, headaches and migraines, dry eyes and mouth, rashes and other skin problems, vision problems, and poor coordination. The causes of fibromyalgia are unknown, and there is currently no lab test that can diagnose the condition.

In a recent study of 336 adults, published in the Journal of Clinical Psychiatry, those with fibromyalgia were almost seven times more likely to have suffered from an anxiety disorder than those without fibromyalgia. They were also about three times more likely to have suffered major depression than those who had not experienced fibromyalgia. The study found the onset of an anxiety disorder or other mental illness in people with fibromyalgia preceded the onset of the fibromyalgia, suggesting that anxiety or depression may be more than just a reaction to the chronic pain. The researchers noted there may be a "shared vulnerability" between the psychiatric disorders and fibromyalgia, possibly genes or environmental factors such as chronic stress. However, the connection remains unknown and requires further study.

Migraine—A migraine is severe pain felt on one or both sides of the head. The pain normally occurs around the temples or behind one eye or ear. A migraine may also cause nausea and vomiting and sensitivity to light and sound. The pain can last a few hours or up to two days. In a classic migraine a person experiences an aura, or visual symptoms such as losing vision or seeing flashing lights 10 to 30 minutes before an attack. During a common migraine a person may have nausea, vomiting, or other symptoms, but does not experience an aura.

Migraines (as well as chronic daily headaches) are highly prevalent in people with anxiety disorders, as well as those with mood- and substance-abuse disorders. Many studies have found that generalized anxiety disorder and panic disorder are particularly associated with migraines or other types of headaches. Moreover, in people with a co-occurring anxiety disorder and migraines, the likelihood of major depression increases. As with fibromyalgia, researchers have suggested that there may be a common predisposition to anxiety disorders, depression, and migraines.

Back Pain—Anxiety disorders and back pain often co-occur; back pain is more common in people with anxiety and mood disorders than those without them. Illness, accidents, and infections are among the causes of back pain. According to WebMD, no matter the cause, back pain symptoms are the same, and they include persistent aches or stiffness anywhere along the spine; sharp, localized pain in the neck, upper back, or lower back, especially after lifting heavy objects or engaging in strenuous activity; and chronic ache in the middle or lower back, especially after sitting or standing for extended periods.

An anxiety problem and a co-occurring chronic pain condition can make a person's health more difficult to treat. But a variety of treatments and lifestyle changes can offer relief. Here are some possible health complications:

- Increased disability or reduced functioning
- Poorer quality of life
- Poorer response to treatment
- Poorer treatment follow-through including medication management
- Increased perception of disease severity

People living with chronic pain who also have an anxiety problem often experience lower pain tolerance or a lower pain threshold. People with an anxiety condition may be more sensitive to medication side effects or more fearful of harmful side effects of medication than people who aren't anxious, and they may also be more fearful of pain than someone who experiences pain without anxiety.

Recommended Treatment Interventions for People with an Anxiety Problem and Chronic Pain

According to the Anxiety Disorders Association of America (ADAA), a comprehensive plan with a number of treatment components is necessary to treat people with anxiety and chronic pain. A physician will work with a patient to develop a treatment approach tailored to specific conditions and symptoms. Below is more information about some treatment options recommended by the ADAA for people experiencing anxiety disorders and chronic pain.

Cognitive-Behavioral Therapy (CBT)—CBT helps patients identify, challenge, and change unwanted and unproductive thoughts and feelings, as well as modify and gain control over unwanted behavior. The patient learns recovery skills that are useful for a lifetime. CBT is used to treat both anxiety disorders and chronic pain conditions.

Medication—Very useful in the treatment of anxiety disorders and chronic pain, medication is often used in conjunction with therapy and other treatment techniques. Depending on the individual, medication may be either a short-term or long-term treatment option. The choice of medication should be discussed thoroughly between doctor and patient, and it will always depend on individual circumstances. Some people with an anxiety disorder and chronic pain may be able to find one medication that helps alleviate the symptoms of both conditions. Others may take one medication for anxiety and another for pain management.

Relaxation Techniques—Relaxation techniques may help individuals develop the ability to cope more effectively with the stresses that contribute to anxiety and pain. Common techniques include breathing retraining, progressive muscle relaxation, and exercise.

Complementary and Alternative Methods—Yoga, acupuncture, therapeutic massage, and biofeedback (controlling how the body reacts to stress to reduce its effects) are among the complementary and alternative techniques that relieve the symptoms of both anxiety disorders and chronic pain.

Basic Lifestyle Changes Recommended for People Living with an Anxiety Disorder and Chronic Pain

Many lifestyle changes that improve the symptoms of an anxiety disorder also help the symptoms of chronic pain. Below is more information about some areas of change recommended by the ADAA for people experiencing anxiety disorders and chronic pain.

Good Nutrition—Nutrition and diet can influence both anxiety and chronic pain symptoms. People with anxiety should limit or avoid caffeine and alcohol, which can trigger panic attacks and worsen anxiety symptoms. According to the National Fibromyalgia Association, certain foods aggravate some musculoskeletal conditions; they include dairy products, gluten (found in wheat, oats, barley, and rye), corn, sugar, and members of the nightshade family (potatoes, tomatoes, eggplant, peppers, and tobacco). The association recommends that individuals who experience pain reduce their intake of tea, coffee, alcohol, red meat and other acid-forming foods. A doctor can provide patients with more guidance on foods to eat regularly and those to avoid.

Exercise—Regular exercise produces many positive effects for people with anxiety disorders and chronic pain. It strengthens muscles, reduces stiffness, improves flexibility, and boosts mood and self-esteem. Some people with chronic pain find exercising difficult to do, but because it often helps reduce overall pain, its benefits may be worth any temporary discomfort. All individuals, particularly those with chronic pain, should check with their doctors before beginning an exercise regimen.

Sleep Management—Getting a good night's sleep is key for anxiety disorders and chronic pain conditions. Symptoms of both types of conditions often become worse without proper or enough sleep. Consistent sleep and wake times, a good sleep environment (comfortable room temperature, no TV or other distractions), and avoiding caffeine late in the day and at night can help promote restful sleep.

The Role of Sleep Disturbances in Chronic Pain Management

Over the years I have found that one problem common

to most of my patients living with chronic pain is that they experience problems sleeping. For some it is minor, but for others it becomes debilitating. According to the National Sleep Foundation two-thirds of people living with chronic pain experience sleep problems. Only about 15 percent of all people have sleep problems. Compounding the problem of disturbed sleep in people who hurt is the fact that some chronic pain medications can disrupt sleeping patterns.

In one study, approximately two-thirds of patients with chronic back pain suffered from sleep problems. Research has demonstrated that disrupted sleep will, in turn, exacerbate chronic back pain. Thus, a vicious cycle develops in which the back pain disrupts one's sleep, and difficulty sleeping makes the pain worse, which in turn makes sleeping more difficult, etc.

Difficulty Falling Asleep

Chronic pain can impact sleep in a number of ways. To understand how pain can make it difficult to fall asleep, think about the processes associated with going to sleep for the night.

In getting ready for bed, it is common to eliminate all distractions or other influences in an effort to "relax" and fall asleep. This may include quieting the room, turning off the lights, eliminating any other noises, trying to get comfortable so that you can begin to fall asleep.

However, this "quieting" of one's environment can cause problems for the person living with chronic pain since the only thing left for the brain to focus on is the experience of pain. People will often report that one of their primary pain management tools during the day is being able to distract themselves from their chronic pain by staying busy with other tasks (for example, reading, watching television, engaging in hobbies or crafts, working, interacting with others). In many cases, one's perception of pain actually increases when attempting to fall asleep. The longer falling asleep is delayed, the more stressful the situation becomes.

Difficulty Sleeping through the Night

People with chronic pain who have a difficult time falling asleep, also report waking up frequently during the night. Research has shown that individuals experiencing chronic lower back pain may experience several intense "micro-arousals" (a change in sleep state to a lighter stage of sleep) per hour of sleep, which lead to awakenings. Thus, a chronic pain problem can be a significant intrusion into a night's sleep and disruptive to the normal stages of sleep.

This problem is often the cause of "non-restorative sleep." Individuals with chronic pain experience less deep sleep, more arousals and awakenings during the night, as well as less efficient sleep. Thus, the quality of the sleep is often light and not refreshing. This non-restorative sleep pattern can then cause diminished energy, depressed mood, fatigue, and worse pain during the day.

One of my former patients, George, had only been sleeping two to three hours per day for several months when he came to my practice. This sleep deprivation was causing major problems with his thinking and emotional management, as well as negatively impacting his pain management. For him it was a depressing cycle—he hurt so he couldn't sleep; when he couldn't sleep he hurt more; when he hurt more he couldn't sleep.

The consequences of sleep deprivation include physical effects, mental impairment, and mental health complications. Inadequate rest impairs our ability to think, to handle stress, to cope with pain, to maintain a healthy immune system, and to moderate our emotions. Total sleep deprivation is fatal: lab rats denied the chance to rest, die within two to three weeks.

Other people who take medications for pain and sleep

may end up going to the other end of the sleep disorder spectrum. My patient Sara was so heavily medicated that her family became concerned. She would sleep 18–20 hours per day and was still groggy. It turned out she was heavily overmedicated.

The New York Times reports that about 42 million prescriptions for sleep medication were issued in 2005. Aside from being overprescribed, sleep medications these days can have strange side effects such as sleep-driving!

For George and Sara the solution was a biopsychosocial treatment plan that included more effective medication management, and as a result both experienced significant quality of life improvements. In addition to medication management, an important part of improving their quality of sleep was practicing good sleep hygiene.

Developing Good Sleep Hygiene

So what do you do when you live with chronic pain and need to sleep? Do you give in and use potentially dangerous sleep medications or just suffer?

Most experts say understanding the cause of their sleep problem, and practicing good sleep hygiene leads to a better quality of life. Sleep hygiene refers to the habits, environmental factors, and practices that may influence the length and quality of your sleep which include bedtime rituals and other disruptions. Sleep hygiene is typically represented by simple guidelines meant to effectively promote a good night's rest, such as the following:

• Relax before bedtime
• Make sure your bedroom is quiet, dark, cool, and comfortable
• Make sleep a priority; don't sacrifice sleep to do daytime activities
• Get up and go to bed at the same time every day, even on weekends

- Avoid caffeine and other stimulants
- Don't smoke—in bed or at all
- Exercise every day, but avoid doing it four hours before bedtime
- Bedrooms are for sleeping and sex, not for watching television or doing work
- Don't toss and turn
- Don't take naps

I've been helping people with this problem for a long time and have actually used most of interventions listed above. One of the tools I also recommend for many of my patients is the use of headphones with relaxation techniques, soothing sounds or music to help them sleep. I also teach people relaxation response techniques that take about 7–10 minutes and one of the positive side effects is a reduction in their perception of pain. If sleep problems persist after implementing sleep hygiene practices, it may be time to seek medical help.

The Role of PTSD in Chronic Pain Management

Coping with chronic pain can be a difficult struggle that requires a lifestyle management approach focused on caring for your body, mind, and spirit. This is even more difficult if the cause of your pain involves a trauma, such as a motor vehicle accident, work-related injury, combat-related injury, assault, or even complications from a surgical procedure.

In some cases, a person who is exposed to a traumatic event can develop an intense fear response to the trauma—a psychological syndrome called post-traumatic stress disorder (PTSD). There is research and clinical practice evidence to suggest an interaction between pain and PTSD, since they frequently co-occur and can interact in such a way to negatively impact the course of treatment for either condition. Given the high rates of people experiencing chronic pain and PTSD, efforts to develop more effective treatments are greatly needed.

It is important to recognize that certain types of chronic pain are more common in individuals who have experienced specific traumas. For example, adult survivors of physical, psychological, or sexual abuse tend to be more at risk for developing certain types of chronic pain later in their lives. The most common forms of chronic pain for survivors of these kinds of trauma involve: pain in the pelvis, lower back, face, and bladder; fibromyalgia; interstitial cystitis; and whiplash symptoms that never go away.

Some of the theories as to why this relationship occurs relate to personality development, neurobiology or neurophysiology, memory, behavior, and personal coping styles. If you have a history of any type of trauma, it is essential that you give your healthcare providers accurate information about your experiences.

The prevalence of PTSD has been estimated to be between 20 to 34 percent in patients referred for the treatment of pain. The prevalence of pain has been estimated to be between 45 to 87 percent in patients referred for the treatment of PTSD. Data obtained from VA Boston Healthcare System Pain Management Psychology Services indicates that 50 percent of patients assessed met the criteria for PTSD based on PTSD checklist scores.

Patients living with both chronic pain and PTSD experience more intense pain, more emotional distress, higher levels of life interference, and greater disability than people without PTSD. Due to the interaction of these conditions, their pain situation can also be more complex and challenging to treat.

Because research has shown that individuals with PTSD who develop chronic pain experience greater difficulty coping with pain, higher levels of pain and distress, and greater interference of pain in their lives than people who have no

PTSD symptoms, it is very important to get a PTSD assessment if you have an injury-related pain condition.

Some PTSD Symptoms

- A person is exposed to a traumatic event that involves experiencing or witnessing an actual or threat of death or serious injury.
- The person may begin to re-experience the event with reoccurring dreams and/or intrusive thoughts or "flashbacks" that can be very stressful.
- The person may avoid thoughts, feelings, activities, people, and places that remind him or her of the trauma. She or he may even avoid talking about the trauma or steer clear of the site of the accident or incident because it is too upsetting.
- The person may have difficulty falling or staying asleep, irritability and anger, difficulty concentrating, an exaggerated response to sudden loud noises or movements, and extreme watchfulness.

Individuals may begin to experience these symptoms immediately after a trauma or even months afterward (called delayed onset). While some people who develop these symptoms recover within a few weeks or months, others may continue to experience symptoms longer than three months and even years later which then becomes chronic PTSD.

Relationship between Chronic Pain and PTSD

While chronic pain and PTSD are conditions that may occur together, their relationship to one another is not always obvious and often goes unnoticed. PTSD can be overlooked because you, your healthcare provider, and your family may be focused on your pain condition. At times, your level of disability may be attributed solely to pain. Because there is such a close relationship between PTSD and chronic pain, they have been referred to as *mutually maintaining* conditions. This is because the presence of both PTSD and chronic pain can increase the symptom severity of either condition.

For example, people with chronic pain may avoid activity because they fear the pain—avoiding activity can lead to physical deconditioning and greater disability and increased pain over time. Similarly, people with PTSD may avoid reminders of the trauma. This avoidance of activity can lead to the continuation of PTSD symptoms while also contributing to greater physical disability.

People with chronic pain may also focus their attention on their pain while individuals with PTSD may unknowingly focus on things that remind them of the trauma. Consequently, people with both PTSD and chronic pain may have less time and energy to focus on more adaptive ways of coping with both their pain and fear. People with PTSD often experience symptoms of being overexcited and experience significant tension, which may decrease their tolerance for handling pain and increase their perception of pain.

In the following table are recommendations for healthcare providers that were developed for the National Center for PTSD by Lorie T. DeCarvalho, PhD. You might want to review these recommendations and your reactions to this information with your pain management team.

> When patients are coping with a chronic pain condition, it is difficult for them to hear from a healthcare provider that they will need to "live with it" and "manage the pain" for the rest of their lives. Being faced with the news of impending health problems, ongoing severe pain, and disability is extremely difficult. These individuals may have lost their physical abilities, and they have lost the assurance that they can fully control whatever is going on in their lives. Much like losing a loved one, these individuals will need to grieve their losses. This may take some time and will

vary from person to person. Here are some suggestions for assisting these individuals:

- Gather a thorough biopsychosocial history and assess the individual for medical and psychiatric problems. Do a risk assessment for suicidal and homicidal ideation. Also ask about misuse of substances, such as drugs or alcohol, including over-the-counter and prescription drugs or narcotics. Taking appropriate steps to ensure someone is clean and sober and not using medications or other substances to self-medicate is a necessary component of treatment.

- Assess for PTSD symptoms. A quick screen may involve asking the person these questions: In the past month have you (1) had nightmares about _____ when you didn't want to?(2) tried hard not to think about _____ or gone out of your way to avoid situations that reminded you of _____? (3) been constantly on guard, watchful, or easily startled? or (4) felt numb or detached from others, activities, or your surroundings?

- Make appropriate referrals for PTSD, depression, other psychiatric disorders, or significant spiritual issues. Likewise, help build up or stabilize their social support network, as this will act as a buffer against the stress they are experiencing.

- Understand that prior to patients being able to come to an acceptance about the permanence of their condition, they will be feeling very much out of control and helpless. Their lives essentially revolve around trying to regain their sense of control, and this can sometimes be difficult, particularly when treatments don't seem to help or the patient's support system is weak. There may be times when they become outwardly angry or depressed. Restoring some sense of control and empowering the patient is a fundamental part of the treatment process.

The Role of Stress in PTSD and Chronic Pain Management

Stress management and learning relaxation response techniques are crucial components of a PTSD treatment plan. It is important to educate yourself about the connection between stress levels and pain symptoms, as well as understanding that stress management can also decrease your suffering.

Stress Thermometer		
Trauma Reaction	20	Psychosis/Collapse
	15	Dissociation
	10	Loss of Control
Stress Reaction	9	Overreact
	8	Get Driven/Defensive
	7	Space Out
Functional Reaction	6	Free Flow With Effort
	5	Free Flow With No
	4	Effort
Relaxation	3	Relaxed—Focused
	2	Relaxed—Not Focused
	1	Relaxed—Nearly Asleep

Physically, chronic pain raises stress levels and drains physical energy, while psychologically it affects the ability to think clearly, logically, and rationally, as well as to effectively manage feelings or emotions. Remember that in most cases if you can learn to lower your stress levels, you will also experience a decrease in your perception of pain.

It is important to learn how to self-assess your levels of stress and then learn how to implement simple but effective stress management tools. I like to use the Gorski-CENAPS® Stress Thermometer noted on page 127 to help my patients accurately articulate their level of stress. This concept proposes that there are ten levels of stress; when you get to the moderate to higher levels of stress your thinking and behaviors are impacted.

The goal is to keep your stress in the *Functional Stress* levels of 4–6. When you get up into the *Stress Reaction* levels 7–9, you are not able to focus on much of anything and eventually get upset or angry and say or do things you know you'll regret, but you just can't stop yourself.

When you get to level 10, *Trauma Reaction*, you are at high risk of going out of control and will eventually shut down. There is also a strong correlation between stress and level, or perception, of pain. As stress goes up, the pain experience often worsens, and as pain levels increase, stress also increases—it can become a vicious cycle. You'll learn more about the *Relaxation* level later.

Effectively Using a Pain Journal

Improving Your Relationship with Your Pain

Below you will have an opportunity to gain even more insights about your personal pain relationship. The main purpose of this exercise is for you to gather daily written feedback regarding your internal perception (insights) of your pain condition and how you manage your pain.

You will be looking for triggers (physical, psychological/emotional, and stress triggers) and patterns for your pain. You'll be learning more about pain and suffering in the next chapter, but this is your starting point to begin improving your relationship with pain.

Pain journaling is a common tool used in pain management; many of you have probably already been exposed to it. In the exercise below I will show one of the pain journaling assignments I used effectively with Mary, Mark, and many of my other chronic pain patients. Any type of journaling about pain is useful; this is only one of many techniques you can use to begin the process.

Please Stop and Complete Your First Pain Journaling Exercise by Following the Seven Steps Listed Below

1. In your journal at least two times per day list the type of pain—also note whether it is more physiological or psychological/emotional—and the highest level of pain (using the 0 to 10 pain scale) that you are experiencing and why you rated it that way.

2. Using the stress thermometer also identify the highest level of stress you experienced and why you rated it that way—what were your stress triggers?

3. Note what you do for your pain (for example, medication, stretching, exercise, massage) and how well it works (on 0 to 10 scale with 0 meaning not at all and 10 meaning totally).

4. Identify what you were doing (that day or earlier) that may have triggered the pain or stress and note any ways you could avoid those situations (triggers) in the future. Be sure to include both physical triggers and emotional triggers.

5. Identify any negative (self-defeating or addictive) thoughts you are having because of your pain.

6. Identify any uncomfortable feelings you are having or poor decisions you are making because of your pain.
7. At the end of each day identify the most important thing you learned about your pain and commit to one thing that you will do differently to improve your pain management.

Your Second Step Call to Action

You have now completed the second step of your pain management journey and here is your opportunity to summarize your experience in this step. Please answer the three questions below:

1. What is the most important thing you have learned about yourself and your pain management as a result of completing this step? _____

_____

_____

2. What are you willing to commit to do differently as a result of what you have learned by completing this step?

_____

_____

_____

3. What obstacles might get in the way of your making these changes and what can you do to overcome those roadblocks? _____

_____

_____

**Please Take Time to Pause,
Rest, and Reflect
Then Go on to Step Three**

Step Three:
Exploring Pain versus Suffering

As we talked about in previous sections, the psychological meaning that you assign to a physical pain signal will determine whether you simply feel pain ("Ouch, this hurts!") or experience suffering ("Because I hurt, something awful or terrible is happening!"). Although pain and suffering are often used interchangeably, there is an important distinction that needs to be made. Again, pain is an unpleasant signal telling you that something is wrong with your body; suffering results from the meaning or interpretation your brain assigns to the pain signal—this is your perception of pain.

You Can Change Your Perception of Pain

The Three Parts of Pain

- **Biological:** A signal that something is going wrong with your body

- **Psychological:** The meaning that your brain assigns to the pain signal

- **Social/Cultural:** The approved "sick" role assigned to you by society concerning your pain

Many people irrationally believe that: "I should be able to stop my pain!" or "Because I keep suffering with my pain there must be something wrong with me." A big step toward effective pain management occurs when you can reduce—or even eliminate—your suffering by identifying and changing your irrational thinking and beliefs about pain, which in turn decreases your stress and overall suffering. We'll talk more about this later.

Using a Two-Part Approach: Physiological and Psychological

Because of the two parts—pain and suffering—pain management must also have two components: physical and psychological. The way you sense or experience pain—its intensity and duration—will affect how well you are able to manage it. *Anticipatory pain* (which was covered earlier) is also a major psychological factor that must be addressed.

The research on recovery from chronic pain is very clear. The people that are most likely to successfully manage their pain do so by becoming proactively involved in their own treatment process. The chances of success go up as you learn as much as possible about your pain and effective pain management. One important component to help you succeed is for you to better understand anticipatory pain.

Coping with Anticipatory Pain

When you live with chronic pain, you hurt. Doing certain *things* can make you hurt worse. So you come to believe that these things will *always cause you to hurt.* In other words, you associate those *things* with pain. You believe that every time you do those *things*, you'll have pain.

Because you believe that you're going to hurt, you activate the physiological pain system just by thinking about doing something that you believe will cause you to hurt. This is called *anticipatory pain*. You anticipate that something will make you hurt, which in turn activates the physiological pain system. You start hurting even before you begin doing whatever it is that you believe will cause you to hurt. All you have to do is to start thinking about doing that *thing*.

My pain is horrible, awful, and terrible! I am suffering!

Once the physical pain system is activated, the anticipatory pain reaction can actually make pain symptoms worse. Whenever you feel the pain, you *interpret* it in a way that makes it worse. You *start thinking* about the pain in a way that actually makes it worse. You *tell yourself* the pain is "awful and terrible," and that "I can't handle the pain." You *convince yourself* that "it's hopeless, I'll always hurt, and there's nothing I can do about it."

This dysfunctional way of thinking causes you to develop emotional reactions that further intensify or amplify your pain response. The increased perception of pain causes you to keep changing your behavior in ways that create even more unnecessary limitations and more emotional discomfort. This can make you feel trapped in a progressive cycle of disability.

You get the level of pain and dysfunction that you expect!

Your expectations—what you believe it will be like when you experience pain—does affect your brain chemistry; it can either intensify or reduce the amount of physical pain that you experience. What you think about and how you manage your feelings in anticipation of experiencing pain can make the pain either more severe or less severe. In other words, you usually get the level of pain and dysfunction that you expect—a self-fulfilling prophecy.

The anticipation of an expected pain level can influence the degree to which you experience pain. When your self-talk is saying, "this is horrible, awful, terrible," your brain tends to amplify the pain signals. When this occurs, the level of distress increases—you suffer, remaining a victim to your pain.

Anticipation of pain affects how you experience your pain!

But you can learn how to change your anticipatory response to pain. You can lower the amount of pain that you anticipate by changing what you believe will happen when you start to hurt. You can also change your thinking—or the self-talk—and learn how to better manage your emotions. You can learn new ways of responding to old situations that cause or intensify pain. As you come to believe that you really can do things that will make your pain sensations bearable and manageable, the brain responds by influencing special neurons that reduce the intensity of the pain. As a result, your brain becomes less responsive to an incoming pain signal.

There are things you can do that will make you less responsive to incoming pain signals. Both ascending (pain signals coming from the point of injury to the brain) and descending nerve pathways (signals from the brain to the point of injury) will influence or modify the effects of pain on the body. This is the reason for including biofeedback, positive self-talk, meditation, and relaxation response training as part of your pain management treatment plan.

Moving Beyond Anticipatory Pain

In December of 2007, I wrote an article titled "Coping with Anticipatory Pain." Much of that article's content is in the previous section. This has been one of the most requested articles on our website over the past few years. I now believe it's time to take another step in supporting people to not just cope with anticipatory pain, but to move beyond it.

I learned a long time ago that what we expect is usually what we get, which can be both beneficial and harmful. When it comes to feeling pain and development of an effective chronic pain management plan, it is crucial to understand the role of anticipatory pain. It has both biological and psychological components.

Remember, on the biological side, the cascade of effects from a pain sensation occurs on many levels and involves a variety of different areas within the nervous system. As a result, a wide variety of nervous system chemicals are produced and dumped into the blood while other brain chemicals are rapidly absorbed or depleted. Pain doesn't just hurt—it changes the most basic neurophysiological processes in the human body.

As I mentioned earlier, the psychological side can influence the degree to which you experience your pain, especially anticipation of an expected pain level. In some cases, when your anticipatory level of pain expectation is lowered, your brain responds by influencing special neurons. This renders your brain less responsive to an incoming pain signal and your sensation of pain decreases. In any event, both ascending (pain signals coming from the point of injury to the brain) and descending nerve pathways (signals from the brain to the point of injury) will influence or modify the effects on your body.

The good news is that you can learn how to change your anticipatory pain response. You can lower the amount—or perception—of pain that you anticipate by changing what you believe will happen when you start to hurt. You can also change your thinking, or your self-talk, and learn how to better manage your emotions. You can learn new ways of responding to old situations that used to cause or intensify your pain. As you come to believe that you really can do things that will make your pain sensations bearable and manageable, your brain responds by influencing special neurons that reduce the intensity of your pain. Your brain becomes less responsive to an incoming pain signal.

You can learn to develop new patterns that can make you habitually less responsive to incoming pain signals. Herein lies the rationale for including biofeedback, positive self-talk, meditation, and relaxation response training as part of your pain management treatment plan. In any event, both ascending (pain signals coming from the point of injury to the brain) and descending nerve pathways (signals from the brain to the point of injury) influence or modify the effects of pain on your body.

Remember the important question about learning from pain: What is my pain trying to tell me? Unfortunately, it can sometimes be difficult, if not impossible, to pinpoint the pain generator, and as human beings we want to know why something is happening and we want to know "right now." Because when we're in pain a more important question is: "What do I need to do, right now, to manage my pain in a healthier way that supports me physically, emotionally, and spiritually?" The answer will be different for each person.

Understanding Pain versus Suffering

But what if you can't answer that question because your chronic pain has become unmanageable, no matter what you try? This brings us back to our discussion of pain versus suffering. The psychological meaning you assign to a physical pain signal that determines whether you simply feel pain ("Ouch, this hurts!") or experience suffering ("This pain is awful and will just keep getting worse; this is terrible and why is it happening to me!").

It is crucial to remember that because pain and suffering are often used interchangeably, in order to avoid suffering you need to make the distinction. You need to remind yourself that pain is a physical sensation, a warning sign telling you that something is going on in your body and you need to listen. Suffering results when you amplify or distort this with your thinking and feeling response.

You can develop many mistaken beliefs when you get caught up in the chronic pain trance. Many of those beliefs are what lead you—and keep you—in suffering. A big step toward effective chronic pain management occurs when you can get rid of your suffering by identifying and changing your thoughts and beliefs about your pain, which in turn can decrease your stress, uncomfortable emotions and overall suffering.

The Role of Neuroplasticity

As I mentioned earlier, neuroplasticity refers to the changes that occur in the organization of the brain as a result of experience. As such, brain activity associated with a given function can move to a different location as a consequence of normal experience or brain damage/recovery.

It has now been found that this capacity for rewiring of the neuronal synapses to allow for re-development of entire regions of the brain is present in adults as well as children. Newly discovered principles of neuroplasticity are at the heart of some of the most revolutionary and groundbreaking brain research.

Constantly living in anticipatory pain actually changes your neuronetwork. In addition, learning and practicing ways to change your beliefs, thoughts, and conclusions about pain can change your neuronetwork, so eventually you can move beyond your previous anticipatory pain responses.

Pain research presented by the American Society of Anesthesiologists has emphasized the molecular transduction of painful stimuli, the sensitization processes that occur after injury and long-term phenomena such as pain memory. Neuroplasticity after surgery occurs in the central nervous system, where central sensitization occurs—where the signals are generated.

According to Kenneth Sufka in his article published in *Brain and Mind: A Transdisciplinary Journal of Neuroscience and Neurophilosophy* in 2004:

Pain that persists long after damaged tissue has recovered remains a perplexing phenomenon. This so-called chronic pain serves no useful function for an organism and, given its disabling effects, might even be considered maladaptive. However, a remarkable similarity exists between the neural bases that underlie the hallmark symptoms of chronic pain and those that serve learning and memory. Both phenomena, wind-up in the pain literature and long-term potentiation (LTP) in the learning and memory literature, are forms of neuroplasticity in which increased neural activity leads to a long lasting increase in the excitability of neurons through structural modifications at pre- and post-synaptic sites.

Cognitive-behavioral Restructuring for Reprogramming the Neuronetwork

As my friend and mentor Terry Gorski says, language is the key to reprogramming the neuronetwork. His TFUAR process that I explained in the section entitled "Break Through the Chronic Pain Trance" is a cognitive-behavioral restructuring model for chronic pain management, and is especially useful for moving beyond anticipatory pain.

Back in step one you learned about principles that helped you to better understand how the TFUAR (Thoughts, Feelings, Urges, Actions, and Reactions) process works. I believe it is important to review those principles here in the context of how it can be used to reprogram your neuronetwork.

- **Thoughts and feelings work together to cause urges.** Your way of thinking causes you to feel certain feelings. These feelings, in turn, reinforce the way you are thinking. These thoughts and feelings work together to create an urge, or impulse, to do something. An urge is a desire that may be rational or irrational.

- Sometimes the irrational urge is to isolate and give in to your depression. At other times you might be tempted to use inappropriate chronic pain management medication, including alcohol or other drugs, even though you know it will hurt you, which is also called craving. Other times you want to use self-defeating behaviors that at some level you know will not be good for you and could worsen your depression.

- **Urges plus decisions cause actions.** You need to remember that this decision is a choice. A choice is a specific way of thinking that causes you to commit to one way of action while refusing to do anything else. The space between the urge and the action is always filled with a decision or choice. This decision may be an automatic and unconscious choice that you have learned to make without stopping to think about it, or this decision can be based on a conscious choice that results from carefully reflecting on the situation and the options that are available to you for dealing with it in a better way.

- **Actions cause reactions from other people.** Your actions affect other people and cause them to react to you. It is helpful to think about your behavior like invitations that you give to other people to treat you in certain ways. Some behaviors invite people to be nice to you and to treat you with respect. Unfortunately, many of your old automatic and unconscious behaviors invited people to react to you in a negative manner.

  These old behaviors invite people to argue and fight with you or to put you down. In every social situation you share a part of the responsibility for what happens because you are constantly inviting people to respond to you by the actions you take and how you react to what other people do. Sometimes these reactions help you manage your pain more effectively, but at other times it leads to increased stress levels that cause you to make poor decisions.

This TFUAR process is a suggested starting point to support you in moving beyond anticipatory pain so you can develop a more effective chronic pain management plan.

However, this is only a first step, although a critical one, that needs to be enhanced as you move forward in your chronic pain management journey. Please remember that the anticipatory response can also work for you. If you expect to have success with your chronic pain management that is what you will tend to manifest. You can learn to make this a positive self-fulfilling prophecy and continue to move beyond anticipatory pain.

Stress Management Is Crucial for Effective Chronic Pain Management

In today's busy world it's very important to incorporate effective stress management tools into your daily living. You hear it all the time; phrases like "I'm stressed-out" or "this stress is killing me." This is obviously true for people living with medical conditions like heart disease or diabetes. And, if you're living with chronic pain, it's even more important because increased stress leads to increased pain.

It's important to realize that you need some level of stress to motivate and help you deal with life on life's terms. Stress can also give you energy and fuels the fight, flight, or freeze phenomenon. When you live with a chronic pain condition stress intensifies your experience of pain. The stress response is a combination of biological, psychological, and behavioral factors.

In response to stress, your body mobilizes an extensive array of physiological and behavioral changes in a process of continual adaptation. This is an important part of your body's defenses with the goal of maintaining homeostasis and coping with stress. Your body reacts to stress by secreting two types of chemical messengers—hormones in the blood and neurotransmitters in the brain. That is why stress management needs to be an integral part of an effective chronic pain management program.

Managing Your Stress Helps You Manage Your Pain

It is important to understand the connection between stress levels and pain symptoms, as well as recognizing that stress management can decrease the perception of pain. Physically, chronic pain raises stress levels and drains physical energy. Psychologically, it affects people's ability to think clearly, logically and rationally, as well as to effectively manage their feelings or emotions. Remember, in most cases when someone learns how to lower their stress levels, they will also experience a decrease in their perception of pain.

Of course before someone learns how to manage their stress, they need to know how to assess their level of stress at any given time. It is important to know how to accurately assess stress and then how to implement some simple, but effective, stress management tools. I like using the Gorski-CENAPS® Stress Thermometer you learned about earlier. What is important to remember is when you get to the upper moderate to severe levels of stress (6–10 range or the stress reaction) your thinking, emotions, and behavior are negatively impacted. The goal is to keep your level of stress at six or below as much as possible.

Seven Tips for Effective Stress Management

Here are seven simple tips for managing stress that could significantly improve your chronic pain management:

1. Understanding Stress

It's important to learn about stress and understand the stress scale, and to recognize that stress can either be a positive influence or make your life overly difficult. When looking at stress on a 1 to 10 scale, with 1 meaning you are very relaxed and 10 meaning you can't function or you shut down, the danger zone begins at level 7—stress overload! From levels 7 to 10 you will experience disruptive symptoms. It depends on how you interpret this distress—whether you face the situation with confidence or helplessness. At this point, you could shift into survival mode—fight, flight, or freeze. Any of those three modes will amplify your pain levels. The fight mode leads to anger and attacking others; the flight mode leads to fear and hiding; and the freeze mode leads to depression and immobilization.

2. **Stress Reducing Self-talk and Positive Affirmations**
The premise here is if you change the way you think you will automatically start changing the way you feel. For example, if you're under high stress the thought might be "I can't stand this...I need to escape." This in turn could lead to fear, anger, anxiety, or even cravings to use self-defeating behaviors or even inappropriate pain medication for stress relief. You really can talk yourself into feeling better no matter what's happening around you or to you.

3. **Emotional Management**
If you are undergoing chronic pain management you may be experiencing many types of uncomfortable emotions such as fear, anger, shame, and frustration. Emotional management starts with learning to identify which emotions you are feeling and be able to rate them on a 0 to 10 intensity scale. The next step is to develop early awareness of them and then take immediate action to cope with any uncomfortable feelings before they lead to self-defeating urges. Developing healthy feeling management skills is very important. Learning to share with trustworthy people is one way to deal with uncomfortable emotions. If the feelings are too intense or overwhelming, counseling or therapy may be necessary.

4. **Autogenic Breathing or Breath Self-Regulation**
This is a systematic daily practice of breathing sessions

that last around 15 minutes, usually in the morning, at lunchtime, and in the evening. One simple exercise is to breathe in deeply to the count of five, hold for seven counts, and slowly exhale counting down from nine to zero. You might consider adding this breath exercise to the next stress tip and practice both three times a day.

5. **Progressive Muscle Relaxation**

   One way to do this is by taking slow deep breaths then holding your breath while tensing up one muscle group at a time. When you exhale let the muscle group relax. Then move to the next group and keep going until you are tensing and releasing all the muscle groups in your body.

6. **Meditation**

   There are literally hundreds, if not thousands, of types of meditation. One way is to select a consistent time and a quiet place, either early morning or evening. Wear loose fitting clothing and find a comfortable position that you can stay in for at least 30 minutes. Do deep breathing for a minute or two to help relax the body. Close your eyes and then focus on the point between your eyebrows to help increase your concentration. If your mind wanders, be gentle with yourself and just refocus. When you first start, meditate for five to seven minutes then slowly increase your time.

7. **Exercise and Nutrition**

   A very effective stress management strategy is exercise. In addition to lowering stress levels, regular exercise can also be an important part of a pain management program. Some people with chronic pain find exercising difficult to do, but because it helps reduce overall pain, its benefits will be worth any temporary discomfort. All individuals, particularly someone undergoing chronic pain management, should check with their doctors before beginning an exercise regimen.

Nutrition and diet can influence chronic pain symptoms. Many people find it extremely difficult, but reducing or even eliminating nicotine, caffeine, and sugar will go a long way toward developing a healthy eating plan that can impact pain symptoms. Seeking out an experienced nutritionist can be very beneficial for both stress and chronic pain management.

This Is Just the Starting Point

These seven tips are just a starting point and I encourage you to learn to use as many other stress management tools as you can. When you are more aware of your stress levels, you will feel more empowered to take action to reduce the stress in your life, which in turn leads to a decrease in your pain symptoms—your perception of pain.

My call to action for anyone undergoing chronic pain management is to implement a proactive and strategic stress management plan. Doing so will improve your health and quality of life and most importantly reduce the severity of your pain symptoms.

Because pain is a very subjective experience, there is no instrument that can medically measure your pain. However, in a following exercise you'll get a chance to determine how much of your pain is biological and how much is psychological/emotional. To get the most out of the upcoming exercise I will remind you that you must be totally honest with yourself and circle all the words you use (or could use) to describe your pain to someone else.

But before you go to that exercise, you first need to learn how to effectively use a 0 to 10 pain scale—with 0 being the total absence of any pain signal to 10 being the worst pain you ever experienced.

Using a Pain Scale Effectively

In addition to being able to rate your level of stress, it

is also important to be able to accurately rate your level of pain. Many people I have worked with over the years have consistently rated their pain at levels 9 or 10 on the 0 to 10 pain scale. Part of this high rating may have been a misunderstanding of the pain scale. Another reason, according to some of my patients who finally confided in me, was that they rated it that way so other people would take them seriously or give them something to help them better manage their pain.

Below is a 0 to 10 pain scale that might help you better evaluate your pain so you can let others know what level your pain is at. It will also help you more accurately rate your pain levels in the next exercise.

Understanding the 0–10 Pain Scale

0   =   The absence of any pain signals.

1–3   =   When I have pain at this level, my pain is a nuisance but I can almost always function normally without any extra effort. At these levels I might describe my pain as mildly troubling or irritating, but no big deal. In fact, most of the time I might not even notice that I'm in pain.

4–6   =   When I experience this level of pain, at times I can function normally with extra effort and at other times I struggle. At this level I might describe my pain as frustrating or even aggravating. When my pain gets to level six it starts to feel like a big deal and I'm always conscious of being in pain.

7–10   =   When I reach this level of pain, most of the time I can't function normally even with medication and extra effort. At this level I'm truly "suffering" and here I might describe my pain as awful, horrible, or unbearable. When my pain gets to the 9–10 levels I sometimes panic and mistakenly believe that it will never get better.

Remember, pain levels tend to fluctuate—pain can ebb and flow—like the ocean tides. Different physical and psychological situations can either amplify or sometimes even lower your pain levels. I would also encourage you to develop your own descriptive phrase to describe each of the ten levels of pain on the scale.

Another way to look at describing your pain is by using a brief 10-point scale like the one listed in the table below. As you review this 10-point scale please think how you would describe each of the ten levels in your own words. The important thing is for you to learn how to communicate your levels of pain accurately to your healthcare provider.

Level 1	=	My Pain Is Barely Noticeable
Level 2	=	My Pain Is Noticeable with No Distress
Level 3	=	My Pain Is Becoming Disturbing But No Distress
Level 4	=	My Pain Has Some Distress But No Coping Problems
Level 5	=	My Pain Has Distress with Some Coping Problems
Level 6	=	My Pain Has Distress with Significant Coping Problems
Level 7	=	My Pain Is Starting to Interfere with My Ability to Function
Level 8	=	My Pain Is Causing Moderate Interference with My Ability to Function
Level 9	=	My Pain Is Causing Severe Interference with My Ability to Function
Level 10	=	I'm Unable to Function at All Because of My Pain

Take a few minutes right now to write down how you would describe each of the ten levels of pain in your own words. Try to keep your descriptions brief and concise. The words you choose should let you accurately communicate with others what your pain is like for you at each level.

Now that you understand the role of stress and how to better use the pain scale, it's time to go to the next exercise that is designed to describe and rate the severity of your pain symptoms. Remember, in order to get the most out of the following exercise you must be willing to be objective and very honest with yourself. But before you complete the exercise yourself, please review how Mary and Mark completed their exercises. The symptoms they chose will be in **bold** type.

Mary's Pain Symptoms on a Bad Pain Day

Symptom	Level	Symptom	Level
1. Aching, **throbbing, pulsing**	9	10. **Worrisome, saddening**, depressing	10
2. **Irritating**, nagging, **disturbing**	10	11. **Inflamed**, sharp, **swollen**	8
3. Splitting, **piercing**, pounding	8	12. **Torturing**, grueling, **punishing**	10
4. **Dreadful, severe, awful**	10	13. Hot, **radiating**, spreading	8
5. Irritated, **sore**, sensitive	9	14. Annoying, **upsetting, aggravating**	10
6. Uncomfortable, **troublesome, problematic**	10	15. Tearing, **wrenching**, slashing	8
7. **Burning, stinging**, lacerating	8	16. **Frightening, terrifying, dreadful**	10
8. **Distressing, excruciating, agonizing**	10	17. **Numbing, tingling**, shooting	8
9. Tender, **painful, hurtful**	10	18. **Exhausting**, fatiguing, **debilitating**	10

Mark's Pain Symptoms on a Bad Pain Day

Symptom	Level	Symptom	Level
1. **Aching**, throbbing, pulsing	7	10. **Worrisome, saddening, depressing**	10
2. Irritating, **nagging, disturbing**	8	11. **Inflamed, sharp**, swollen	7
3. Splitting, **piercing**, pounding	6	12. Torturing, grueling, **punishing**	10
4. Dreadful, **severe, awful**	8	13. **Hot**, radiating, **spreading**	6
5. **Irritated, sore**, sensitive	7	14. **Annoying**, upsetting, **aggravating**	8
6. **Uncomfortable, troublesome**, problematic	9	15. **Tearing**, wrenching, slashing	7
7. **Burning**, stinging, **lacerating**	6	16. **Frightening**, terrifying, dreadful	10
8. **Distressing**, excruciating, **agonizing**	9	17. Numbing, tingling, **shooting**	8
9. **Tender, painful**, hurtful	7	18. **Exhausting, fatiguing**, debilitating	10

Both Mary and Mark answered questions 19–20 as all the time because day or night they were constantly in pain with only brief periods of the levels dropping a few points on the 1–10 pain scale after taking their *breakthrough* medication.

Please Go to the Next Section to Identify and Rate the Severity of Your Pain Symptoms

Identifying and Rating the Severity of Your Pain

When you have chronic pain you are the only one that knows how it feels to you. Below are many different words (symptoms) that people with chronic pain use to describe their pain. Not all of these words will apply to you but many of them will. The purpose of this worksheet is twofold: to help you build a vocabulary for talking about your pain, and to rate the intensity of your pain. As you read through each set of groups of symptoms below please circle the **word(s)** and the following **number** that best describe your pain on a **bad pain day.**

	Low Pain		Somewhat Painful				Worst Pain Ever		
1. Aching, throbbing, pulsing	1	2	3	4	5	6	7	8	9	10
2. Irritating, nagging, disturbing	1	2	3	4	5	6	7	8	9	10
3. Splitting, piercing, pounding	1	2	3	4	5	6	7	8	9	10
4. Dreadful, severe, awful	1	2	3	4	5	6	7	8	9	10
5. Irritated, sore, sensitive	1	2	3	4	5	6	7	8	9	10
6. Uncomfortable, troublesome, problematic	1	2	3	4	5	6	7	8	9	10
7. Burning, stinging, lacerating	1	2	3	4	5	6	7	8	9	10
8. Distressing, excruciating, agonizing	1	2	3	4	5	6	7	8	9	10
9. Tender, painful, hurtful	1	2	3	4	5	6	7	8	9	10
10. Worrisome, saddening, depressing	1	2	3	4	5	6	7	8	9	10
11. Inflamed, sharp, swollen	1	2	3	4	5	6	7	8	9	10
12. Torturing, grueling, punishing	1	2	3	4	5	6	7	8	9	10
13. Hot, radiating, spreading	1	2	3	4	5	6	7	8	9	10
14. Annoying, upsetting, aggravating	1	2	3	4	5	6	7	8	9	10
15. Tearing, wrenching, slashing	1	2	3	4	5	6	7	8	9	10
16. Frightening, terrifying, dreadful	1	2	3	4	5	6	7	8	9	10
17. Numbing, tingling, shooting	1	2	3	4	5	6	7	8	9	10
18. Exhausting, fatiguing, debilitating	1	2	3	4	5	6	7	8	9	10

19. Is your pain more (A) permanent, constant, ceaseless; (B) fleeting, brief, momentary; or (C) a combination of both?

20. Why did you rate #19 that way? _____

Ascending and Descending Pain Signals

Ascending pain signals, coming from the point of injury to the brain, and descending nerve pathways, signals from the brain to the point of injury, will influence or modify the effects of pain on your body.

Some of these ascending signals simply report the presence of pain ("I hurt" or "I don't hurt"). Other signals report the intensity of the pain ("it hurts a little" or "it hurts a lot"). Still other pain signals report the location of the pain ("my stomach hurts") or whether the pain is associated with an internal or external injury ("my stomach hurts deep in my gut" or "the skin on my stomach hurts"). Other pain signals report the type of pain ("it burns" or "it throbs").

All of these different pain signals are transmitted into the spinal cord through nerve pathways to the *thalamus* section of the brain. From there the brain transmits the pain signal information to other specialized pain neurons, which in turn send the information (descending signals) to different areas in the brain.

One signal goes to your frontal lobes—this is the cognition/thinking center of the brain. It leads to thoughts or judgments about your pain, including anticipatory pain. From there a signal is sent to another area that gets the pain message, your limbic system—this is the emotional center of the brain. It leads to a feeling or emotional response.

Once the physical pain system is activated, the anticipatory pain reaction can actually make your pain symptoms worse. Whenever you feel the pain, you interpret it in a way that makes it worse. You start thinking about the pain in a way that makes it worse. You tell yourself that the pain is "awful and terrible," and think, "I can't handle the pain." You convince yourself, "It's hopeless, I'll always hurt, and there's nothing I can do about it."

It's very important to remember that when you have pain, there are three components to that pain: (1) biological; (2) psychological/emotional; and (3) social/cultural. All three components need to be treated, but the treatment plan for each differs. An effective medication management plan coupled with nonpharmacological interventions is the best approach for the biological pain symptoms.

However, using medication for the psychological/emotional symptoms is like having an infected cut on your hand and the only thing you do for it is find a color-coordinated bandage and slap it on. Using medication for the psychological/emotional symptoms puts you at risk for experiencing negative side effects from your medication, including potential addiction problems. The good news is there are ways you can learn to identify and cope with your psychological/emotional symptoms. It is also important to identify any social and/or cultural beliefs and biases that could potentially sabotage an effective pain management plan.

Below are the same pain symptoms you identified and rated earlier, but in a slightly different format. Here you have an opportunity to identify your *ascending* and *descending* pain signals. Please take a few minutes to circle the symptoms and numeric ratings from that earlier section. Then add up the total of the levels for each column. But, before you complete your own rating, you might want to review Mary's and Mark's *Ascending/Descending* exercises.

**Please Go to the Next Section
and See How Mary and Mark Scored
Their Ascending and Descending
Pain Signals**

Mary's Ascending/Descending Pain Signals

Ascending/Biological	Level	Descending/Psychological	Level
Aching, **throbbing**, **pulsing**	9	Irritating, nagging, **disturbing**	10
Splitting, **piercing**, pounding	8	**Dreadful, severe, awful**	10
Irritated, **sore**, **sensitive**	9	Uncomfortable, **troublesome**, problematic	10
Burning, stinging, lacerating	8	**Distressing, excruciating, agonizing**	10
Tender, **painful, hurtful**	10	**Worrisome, saddening, depressing**	10
Inflamed, sharp, **swollen**	8	**Torturing**, grueling, **punishing**	10
Hot, **radiating**, spreading	8	Annoying, **upsetting, aggravating**	10
Tearing, **wrenching**, slashing	8	**Frightening, terrifying, dreadful**	10
Numbing, tingling, shooting	8	**Exhausting, fatiguing, debilitating**	10
Total Ascending	= 76	Total Descending	= 90

Mark's Ascending/Descending Pain Signals

Ascending/Biological	Level	Descending/Psychological	Level
Aching, throbbing, pulsing	7	Irritating, **nagging, disturbing**	8
Splitting, **piercing**, pounding	6	Dreadful, **severe, awful**	8
Irritated, sore, sensitive	7	Uncomfortable, **troublesome**, problematic	9
Burning, stinging, **lacerating**	6	**Distressing**, excruciating, agonizing	9
Tender, painful, hurtful	7	**Worrisome, saddening, depressing**	10
Inflamed, sharp, swollen	7	Torturing, grueling, **punishing**	10
Hot, radiating, **spreading**	6	**Annoying**, upsetting, aggravating	8
Tearing, wrenching, slashing	7	**Frightening**, terrifying, dreadful	10
Numbing, tingling, **shooting**	8	**Exhausting, fatiguing**, debilitating	10
Total Ascending	= 61	Total Descending	= 82

What Do Mary's and Mark's Answers Mean?

Several points stand out when reviewing Mark's completed exercise. Mark scored significantly higher in the *descending* area, which is not uncommon for someone living with chronic pain and a coexisting addiction. Mark's first reaction was that he was being manipulated and tricked. This also is a common reaction, especially for patients who have trust issues. Mark eventually learned to use the ascending/descending process as a part of his daily pain journal work.

Psychological/emotional pain is real!
It requires appropriate interventions.

Now let's review Mary's answers for the same exercise. As with Mark, several points stand out when looking through Mary's completed exercise, including the fact that she scored higher in the *descending* area. The first important observation about Mary's descending symptoms is that she scored them **all** at a level 10. There are several reasons this happens for people; the most important is that they have not yet been taught how to understand and complete a pain rating scale.

Please Go to the Next Section
and Score Your Ascending
and Descending Pain Signals

Scoring Your Ascending and Descending Pain Signals

Ascending/Descending Pain Signals		
Ascending/Biological	**Level**	**Descending/Psychological Level**
Aching, throbbing, pulsing		Irritating, nagging, disturbing
Splitting, piercing, pounding		Dreadful, severe, awful
Irritated, sore, sensitive		Uncomfortable, troublesome, problematic
Burning, stinging, lacerating		Distressing, excruciating, agonizing
Tender, painful, hurtful		Worrisome, saddening, depressing
Inflamed, sharp, swollen		Torturing, grueling, punishing
Hot, radiating, spreading		Annoying, upsetting, aggravating
Tearing, wrenching, slashing		Frightening, terrifying, dreadful
Numbing, tingling, shooting		Exhausting, fatiguing, debilitating
Total Ascending =		**Total Descending =**

Are You Willing to Learn More?

Everyone will have both ascending and descending pain signals and many people find that the descending (psychological/emotional) symptoms are significantly higher than the ascending (physiological) symptoms. As I mentioned before, the good news is there are tools you can use to identify and cope with your psychological/emotional symptoms. It is also important to identify any social or cultural beliefs and biases that could potentially sabotage an effective pain management plan.

Please take a few minutes to write in your journal. Write what you learned from this past exercise and how your new understanding can help you better manage your pain.

Your Third Step Call to Action

You have now completed the third step of your pain management journey and here is your opportunity to summarize your experience in this step. Please answer the three questions below:

1. What is the most important thing you have learned about yourself and your pain management as a result of completing this step?

_____

_____

_____

_____

2. What are you willing to commit to do differently as a result of what you have learned by completing this step?

_____

_____

_____

_____

_____

3. What obstacles might get in the way of your making these changes and what can you do to overcome those roadblocks?

_____

_____

_____

_____

**Please Take Time to Pause, Rest,
and Reflect Then Go on to Step Four**

Step Four:
Developing a Successful Pain Management Plan

What Is Effective Chronic Pain Management?

Given the biopsychosocial nature of chronic pain conditions it is imperative to utilize a multidisciplinary treatment plan for effective pain management. Living with chronic pain is very difficult. As I mentioned in the first chapter, if you also have a coexisting addiction or other psychological conditions it becomes even harder. People with chronic pain and coexisting disorders can become severely depressed and feel hopeless. Their self-esteem is practically non-existent and many of them lose the support of their significant others.

Healthcare providers often become confused and frustrated when their treatment interventions are ineffective. Also, we must warn people living with chronic pain not to be fooled by health practitioners who claim to do pain management, yet only do one major thing for your pain, such as medication management, or chiropractic adjustments or acupuncture.

True multidisciplinary pain management involves interventions such as physical therapy, massage, medication management, counseling or therapy, biofeedback, occupational therapy, exercise physiology, an anesthesiologist or pharmacologist, and a case manager all at one site, at a minimum. It may also involve some type of movement therapy such as tai chi, classes on spiritual wellness, yoga or meditation.

In my experience, a multidisciplinary team is crucial in order to address the specific biopsychosocial needs of people living with chronic pain. In addition, the physical, psychological, and social implications of chronic pain and any coexisting condition—including the impact on family systems—must also be adequately dealt with.

It is also essential to implement a collaborative three-part approach: (1) A medication management plan—in consultation with an addiction medicine specialist if abuse or addiction are an issue; (2) A cognitive-behavioral treatment plan—addressing pain versus suffering, treating family system issues and changing self-defeating behaviors; and (3) A nonpharmacological pain management plan—developing safer medication-free ways to manage pain. Recovery and avoiding relapse are possible if patients are willing to do the footwork and utilize a collaborative multidisciplinary treatment team.

Using a multidisciplinary team is crucial when treating the synergistic problems people and their families' face that have been severely impacted by chronic pain, especially when addiction and other psychological problems are present. When these conditions coexist it creates a major challenge that must be addressed through a collaborative treatment approach. The inclusion of addiction, mental health, and medical treatment is vital to this process.

When these coexisting conditions occur, the family problems increase synergistically. Effective treatment can be challenging and confusing for counselors, therapists, and other healthcare providers, but especially for patients and their families. I have found that the strategic three-part approach outlined above improves treatment outcomes and gives people living with chronic pain and their families new hope.

Medication Management

Some pain conditions require pharmacological (prescription drug) interventions. Other conditions may respond to over-the-counter medications like aspirin or ibuprofen. Still other conditions may need a combination of both. Some pain problems can be effectively treated with medication interventions such as acetaminophen and nonsteroidal anti-inflammatory medications, antidepressants, and muscle relaxants.

It is important to remember that for people with a genetic or personal history of an addiction, any psychoactive medication could be problematic. Unfortunately, there may be times when opiate (or opioid) medication management is needed, but there are risks, especially when medication abuse or addiction is an issue.

The Role of Buprenorphine

There's an effective medication for both opiate addiction treatment and/or maintenance chronic pain management. The medication is buprenorphine (Subutex), which is an opiate agonist-antagonist and a very effective pain medication for some people. It has been used in pain management for many years—mostly in its intramuscular (IM) injection form. Buprenorphine is available in the United States as sublingual (dissolved under the tongue) medication and is many times more potent than injected morphine. Buprenorphine is different from other opiates in that you usually feel more "clearheaded" when taking it compared to other opiates.

According to a research study posted in the *American Journal of Occupational Therapy* in 2005, people who failed to achieve lasting analgesia with long-term opioid therapy have achieved benefit using sublingual buprenorphine.

Being the first oral medication that has been approved in the United States, physicians can now prescribe buprenorphine in their offices for people who are dependent or addicted to opiates such as opiate pain medication, heroin, or methadone. Buprenorphine is an effective medication for opiate addiction which does not require daily or weekly visits to a clinic. Buprenorphine blocks the effects of other opiates; it eliminates cravings and prevents withdrawal symptoms such as pain and nausea. Patients can be maintained on buprenorphine or go through detoxification.

Subutex and Suboxone are the brand names that buprenorphine is being marketed under for the treatment of opiate dependence. Both medications contain the active ingredient, buprenorphine hydrochloride, which works to reduce the symptoms of opiate dependence. Subutex contains only buprenorphine hydrochloride which was developed as the initial product.

The second medication, Suboxone contains an additional ingredient called naloxone to guard against misuse or abuse. Subutex is usually given during the first few days of treatment, while Suboxone is used during the maintenance phase of treatment. Both medications come in 2 mg and 8 mg strengths as sublingual (placed under the tongue to dissolve) tablets.

This medication is being used very effectively by some pain management physicians for people living with chronic pain. It is important to remember that medication is only one part of an effective chronic pain management plan. You must also learn to develop nonmedication based treatment interventions as well as how to address the psychological/emotional components of chronic pain. A multidisciplinary team approach always gives the best treatment outcomes.

For someone with chronic pain who has developed an addiction, this medication may be the best intervention possible along with concurrent addiction treatment modalities. In addition, it is important to help people differentiate between the physiological and psychological or emotional components of their pain. Once that is done, cognitive-behavioral approaches can help people manage the psychological components more effectively.

Recovery Friendly or Safer Medications

In my opinion there are no bad medications; however, there are some medications that have negative side effects for some people. It is how the medication is used and who uses it that leads to success or failure. Below is a list of some safer or—for people in recovery from addiction—recovery friendly medications.

- Suboxone or Methadone—for detoxification or transitional chronic pain management
- Celebrex—pre-operation loading; 400 mg before surgical procedures
- All Other NSAIDS—if side effects tolerated
- Sleep Aids
  - Zyprexa 2.5 mg (olanzepine)
  - Rozerem (ramelteon)
- Doxepin (Adapin, Sinequan) for sleep and depression
- Muscle Relaxants *(caution here—can be mood-altering and must be monitored)*
  - Skelaxin (metaxalone)
  - Zanaflex (tizanidine hydrochloride)
  - Robaxin (methocarbamol)
  - Flexeril (cyclobenzaprine hydrochloride)
- Medications for Neuropathic Pain
  - Cymbalta (duloxetine hydrochloride)
  - Lyrica (pregabalin)
- Medications for Migraines
  - Topamax (topiramate)
  - Triptans (serotonin receptor agonists)
  - Toradol IV (ketorolac) for unresponsive pain

- – Zanaflex (tizanidine hydrochloride)
- – Celebrex (celecoxib)
- Ecotrin (coated aspirin—acetylsalicylic acid)
- Anticonvulsants
  - – Tegretol (carbamazepine)
  - – Depakote (divalproex sodium)
- Amitriptyline
- Other Available Medication Classes for Neuropathic Pain
  - – Antidepressants
  - – Antiepileptics such as Neurontin (gabapentin)
  - – Topical analgesics and transdermal patches
  - – Opioids *(often prescribed but not too effective and not that recovery friendly)*
  - – NMDA receptor antagonists
  - – Antispasmodic (magnesium; 400 mg three times a day)
- The Recovery Friendly Patch Delivery Medications
  - – Qutenza (capsaicin)
  - – Lidoderm (lidocaine)
  - – Nonsteroidal anti-inflammatory, such as Voltaren

The Pros and Cons of Acetaminophen

Many people undergoing chronic pain management and on several different medications, including those purchased over the counter, may not realize how much acetaminophen they are really taking. I want to repeat—in my opinion, there is no such thing as a "bad" medication; how it's used and who uses it determines positive or negative outcomes.

To most people, acetaminophen is something of a ubiquitous mystery appearing in many combination cough and cold products as well as many prescription pain medications (such as Vicodin and Percocet). Since many different medications contain this ingredient, consumers may not realize they are taking multiple products that contain acetaminophen, an error that can cause significant liver damage in a very short time.

The maximum daily dosage of acetaminophen historically has been 4,000 mg, and can cause dangerous side effects if people take it in excessive dosages or they have liver disease or drink large amounts of alcohol. In June 2009, the U.S. Food and Drug Administration (FDA) advisory panel voted 21–16 to recommend lowering the maximum daily dose of nonprescription acetaminophen, which at 4,000 mg was equal to eight pills of a drug such as Extra Strength Tylenol.

In addition, the panel voted 24–13 to limit the maximum single dose of acetaminophen to 650 mg. The current single dose of Extra Strength Tylenol, for instance, is 1,000 mg. The panel also voted to make the 1,000 mg dose of acetaminophen available only by prescription. It should be noted that the FDA is not required to accept the panel's recommendations, but it typically does so.

On January 13, 2011, the FDA announced that it is asking manufacturers of prescription acetaminophen combination products to limit the maximum amount of acetaminophen in these products to 325 mg per tablet, capsule, or other dosage unit. The FDA believes that limiting the amount of acetaminophen per tablet, capsule, or other dosage unit in prescription products will reduce the risk of severe liver injury from acetaminophen overdosing, an adverse event that can lead to liver failure, liver transplant, and death. As with earlier recommendations it is requested, not required.

Due to these and other concerns, Johns Hopkins University School of Medicine recommends that even though acetaminophen is the drug with the lowest overall risk of side effects, if someone uses it regularly, they should see their doctor periodically to be monitored for adverse effects.

However, there are many legitimate benefits for using acetaminophen. For example, a 2004 study that was presented at the *9th World Congress of the Osteoarthritis Research Society International (OARSI)* in Chicago showed that the over-the-counter pain reliever acetaminophen, when used as directed, is a safe and effective treatment option for patients suffering from the pain of osteoarthritis of the hip or knee.

According to the results of this study, acetaminophen was found comparable in safety to placebo. There were no statistically significant differences in the number of serious or non-serious adverse events between patients treated with either dose of acetaminophen and placebo. The results of this study confirm that when used as directed, acetaminophen is an effective and safe choice for patients with osteoarthritis and reinforce the *American College of Rheumatology* guidelines that recommend acetaminophen as a first-line therapy to relieve osteoarthritis pain.

Along with its other benefits, acetaminophen is less likely to interact with other medications or irritate the stomach. It is also considered safe for patients with conditions such as heart disease and diabetes.

In the table below is information from the manufacturer of Tylenol (active ingredient acetaminophen) that they posted on their website for people who want—or need—to take it, so they can do so responsibly and safely.

Importantly, you can confidently continue to take TYLENOL according to the directions currently on the package and can prevent inappropriate use by:

- Reading the label before each use and always following the directions
- Never taking more than the recommended dose
- Never using two products containing acetaminophen at the same time
- Keeping medicine out of the reach of children
- Consulting a healthcare professional with questions
- The safety and efficacy of acetaminophen has been established through more than 50 years of clinical use and scientific investigation and it is safe when used as directed.

Any decisions about taking medications should be made with the advice and consultation of an appropriate licensed healthcare provider. I believe that learning as much as possible is one of the most important components of an effective chronic pain management plan.

Remember, effective chronic pain management requires much more than just finding the right medication. In the following sections you will learn more about what it takes to develop a powerful and personal pain management plan. Near the end of the chapter you will be asked to write down your current plan in three areas: (1) Medications; (2) Cognitive-behavioral psychological/emotional tools (i.e., pain versus suffering); and (3) Nonpharmacological interventions. This next section lists twelve of the tools I've helped many of my patients develop over the years.

Twelve Personal Action Steps for Chronic Pain and Medication Management

First of all, I want to emphasize that the information that follows can be used by anyone who wants to avoid prescription medication abuse or addiction problems, not just those already in recovery. Nonetheless, during my career over the past 28 years, I have seen far too many people relapse because of poor medication management plans.

If someone wants to avoid medication abuse or addiction they need a very specific type of primary treatment that addresses coexisting psychological conditions including addiction, as well as relapse prevention protocols that include effective medication management. This type of treatment has always been needed but not really addressed, which is why I developed the *Addiction-Free Pain Management*® *System* and have taught it to healthcare professionals throughout the United States and Canada.

The following suggestions for chronic pain and medication management address not only medication but also other chronic pain interventions that are the result of many years of study, researching literature on outcome-based treatment, and my own personal experience. Along with a friend and colleague, Sheila Thares, RN, MS, APNP, I originally published a pamphlet for people who are in recovery from any type of chemical dependency and living with chronic pain or facing an invasive surgical procedure (medical or dental) that could entail the use of psychoactive medication. Last year we updated the pamphlet and published the new *Addiction-Free Pain Management® Module Four: A Guide for Managing Pain Medication in Recovery*.

As mentioned earlier, an important part of developing an effective chronic pain management plan is to develop an understanding of what an effective plan looks like. I believe it requires a three-part approach that includes effective medication, dealing with the psychological and emotional components of your pain and developing nonmedication based interventions. You also want to remember the importance of working on all four primary areas—biological/physical, psychological, social, and spiritual.

Guidelines for More Effective Chronic Pain Management

Directions: Please use your journal as you read each of the guidelines below and ask yourself how you would rate each of the following areas on a scale of 0 to 10. On this scale zero means that this is something you can't see yourself doing and don't think is important to have on your chronic pain management plan. Ten means this is something you believe is crucial and extremely important for your ongoing effective chronic pain management and are willing to make it part of your plan.

166

1. When under stress or emotional crisis you need to postpone nonurgent dental work (except preventative or restorative) as well as elective surgical procedures requiring additional psychoactive (mood/mind-altering) medications. When you need to be on medication, learn all you can about how to take it safely.

2. If you need to be on potentially addictive medication, have a significant other, or an appropriate support person, hold and dispense the medication. Learn as much as you can about any medication you are prescribed and don't be afraid to ask your prescriber (doctor) questions—be an informed consumer.

3. Consult with a trusted doctor or prescriber about using opiates and other mood/mind-altering medications or even non-addictive medications such as anti-inflammatory or other over-the-counter analgesics—always be open for second opinions.

4. Explore ALL non-mood-altering chronic pain management medications and other modalities, including over-the-counter and prescriptions. Some people find the COX–2 inhibitor non-steroidal anti-inflammatory medications such as Celebrex which does not impede platelets to be helpful. Some of the more common nonpharmacological interventions are acupuncture, chiropractic, physical therapy, massage therapy, and hydrotherapy. If you have neuropathic (nerve) pain, ask your doctor about either Cymbalta or Lyrica. In addition, identifying and managing uncomfortable emotions may decrease your pain significantly.

5. Be aware of your stress levels and have a stress management program already in place such as meditation, exercise, relaxation, music, plenty of rest, and hydration, and relaxation techniques specific to what works for you. If you lower your stress, you will usually lower your pain—or your perception of pain—as a result. When

you experience a pain flare-up your body's automatic response often includes a reflexive tensing response. This problem leads to your being unable to relax the locus of the pain problems, which leads to increased muscle tension in these areas. You need to practice to consciously relax the affected muscles, enabling them to modulate your pain levels and bring the pain under your control without needing to increase your medication.

6. Take personal responsibility to supplement your social support in order to decrease isolation. Take extra precautions about who you share your chronic pain management recovery plan with—not everyone will be supportive of your choices and may even tend to shame you for your choices. Some people find it helpful to join chronic pain management support groups that are available in most communities.

7. The more you focus on your pain, the more you actually intensify your experience of the pain. You need to learn to shift and manipulate your focus of attention in a positive way, which will minimize your experience of the pain. This can be accomplished by changing how you think and feel about your pain. You can then find pleasant activities or tasks to take your focus off your pain.

8. When you are experiencing intense uncomfortable emotions—especially about being in pain—your pain levels actually intensify. Your emotions become like an amplifier circuit that increases the "volume" of your pain. You need to practice specific methods of reducing this automatic process that occurs in the face of stressful triggers. You also need to realize that you may not be able to eliminate these problematic emotional triggers but what you can learn are some different methods of reacting and managing your feelings.

9. Decline "helpful" offers to use someone else's prescriptions. It is crucial to take only your medication as well as

taking it exactly as prescribed. Part of an effective medication management plan is to have a system in place to make sure you take your medications at the right time and the right dose. Some people find the plastic pill dispensing boxes you can get at most pharmacies to be quite helpful.

10. As depression is common for people with chronic pain, consider the possibility of taking appropriate antidepressants if needed. This involves getting a referral to an appropriate mental health professional. The research literature is clear that the best treatment for moderate to severe depression is a combination of appropriate antidepressant medication combined with cognitive-behavioral therapy.

11. Understand the importance of proper exercise as a vital part of chronic pain management. Another problem is that many people experiencing pain flare-ups become very sedentary, with strong avoidance tendencies for many types of activities. The two primary reasons for this are the pain itself, and your own predictions regarding the negative impact of activity. Therefore, it is crucial to return to more normal levels of activities and slowly increase your stamina for physical activities. The primary goal here is to extinguish conditioned avoidance patterns. Implement a stretching program, slowly at first, then structure progressive walking at least once or twice a day if necessary to complete the designated distance. Increase the distance as you are able. Add strengthening exercises if cleared by your MD/NP/PT or other appropriate healthcare provider.

12. Explore your past beliefs and role models from childhood regarding pain and pain management. Look for healthy role models who are effectively managing their chronic pain management condition. Take what you learned from looking at your history and develop an

action plan for moving forward toward more effective chronic pain management.

You can use any of the above 12 suggested steps as your starting point for more effective chronic pain management. To begin, personalize at least three action steps. This is one instance where more is definitely going to be better. Chronic pain management research is clear—people with the best treatment outcomes are active and knowledgeable participants.

Living with Chronic Pain: One Day at a Time

Many of the self-help programs encourage their members to use the slogan "one day at a time." The underlying purpose of this slogan is to help members focus on what needs their time and attention here and now. It encourages people not to be obsessed with their past nor be over-preoccupied with what may happen in the future. This allows them to get the most out of the moment.

Unfortunately, many people misinterpret this slogan in ways that allow them to avoid being proactive about moving out of the problem and into a healthy solution. This refusal to get into action and be proactive is a major stumbling block that I've witnessed in many of my patients. They remain on automatic pilot and just get by. They don't make contingency plans and when an inevitable problem comes up they panic because they don't have a plan in place, then they justify it by claiming they were just following directions and living one day at a time.

My goal is to help you use this slogan to improve your quality of life, not avoid it. If you fail to plan, you may sabotage your chronic pain management plan and experience unnecessary pain flare-ups or other problems.

People undergoing chronic pain management can also

become so hopeless and helpless at times that they mistakenly start believing they are always going to suffer—they get stuck in today only and lose hope. When they are not getting the pain relief they want, they convince themselves life is horrible, awful, and terrible and they deserve to do whatever it takes to feel better. Sometimes that "whatever it takes" leads them to abusing their pain medication.

Another way you can misuse the "one day at a time" slogan is to stop doing what allowed you to manage your pain appropriately and increase the quality of your life. For example, you stop exercising and meditating daily, which leads to the risk of pain flare-ups and a worsening of your condition.

For someone in recovery from an addiction, staying stuck in the moment could lead to a potential relapse which is why I want you to understand the true meaning of living life one day at a time for a better quality of life.

Those who forget the past are doomed to repeat it!

One of the principles underlying this premise is a concept called *timeline competency*—do not become mired in the past, present, or future. You need to first learn how to shift into a peace-centered place by lowering your stress and distress to a manageable level. If you get lost in the shame and guilt or trauma of the past, it destroys your ability to be in a peaceful present. It is important to learn to face the past and learn from it because "those who forget the past are doomed to repeat it."

So, the past is the first area of focus. My goal here is to help you take a look at your history in a safe, supported fashion and see what you can learn. I want to help you discover what you have done well and what your strengths are. The next step is to look for self-defeating patterns of thinking and behaving that caused negative consequences. By doing this, you can begin to learn new healthier ways of coping, so you can plan for a better future.

Covering all the Bases

An important part of developing an effective pain management plan is obtaining an accurate understanding of what effective pain management really means. As mentioned earlier, I believe that effective pain management requires a three-part approach:

1. A medication management plan—developing an effective medication management agreement;

2. A cognitive-behavioral treatment plan—addressing pain versus suffering by better managing your thinking and feelings as well as changing any self-defeating behaviors and problematic social/family reactions; and

3. A nonpharmacological (nonmedication) pain management plan—developing safer ways to manage pain—especially pain flare-ups.

Your Current Pain Management Plan

Before we look into developing such a plan, it is important to first look at what you are currently doing, and have been doing, to manage your pain. Looking back to the first section of this book *Preparing for Your Journey,* it's now time to reorganize that information and to list what you have been doing in each of the three areas above. This is your opportunity to add to and fine-tune your existing pain management plan. Later you will have a chance to further enhance your plan.

• My current medication management plan consists of:

_____

_____

_____

- My cognitive-behavioral (pain versus suffering) plan consists of:

  _____

  _____

  _____

- My nonpharmacological plan consists of:

  _____

  _____

  _____

Refining Your Personal Pain Management Plan

An effective pain management plan starts with an accurate assessment of your presenting problems, your
strengths, weaknesses, support system, as well as any obstacles that could sabotage your pain management. This
usually requires a multidisciplinary approach that includes
an in-depth medical history and physical by your doctor followed by appropriate medical diagnostic testing.

One of the first treatment decisions needs to be whether
or not modification to your medication plan is necessary. If
it is needed, then you need to determine whether asking for
assistance through inpatient medical treatment is necessary
or if you can do it on an outpatient basis with your doctor's
guidance. This is where you develop your personalized appropriate medication management plan—you'll see Mary's
and Mark's revised medication management plans in the
next chapter.

Do You Need Medication Modification?

If modifications to your medications are made, you may
need some craving management tools to help you adhere to
your new plan and ways, in addition to your medication, to
handle pain flare-ups. You'll learn more about medication

management in the next chapter that will help those of you who need additional tools in that area.

Earlier you were taught a way to determine whether your pain is more physiological versus psychological/emotional. This is very important as you implement your pain flare-up management and prevention, so you develop the right type of interventions to help you at that point. Also as you learned earlier, you want to be able to identify and manage any resistance and denial that may have come up regarding pain management and any payoffs for not having an effective pain management plan in place.

You need to develop and implement nonpharmacological pain management interventions. Later in this section you will get a chance to review some common interventions, and develop your own personal plan.

As you continue with your pain management planning it is important to continue learning even more nonpharmacological, holistic pain management tools. Then you need to develop an initial relapse prevention plan that will help you identify your high-risk situations for ineffective pain management or self-sabotage. It is crucial to have a relapse prevention plan in place that addresses both your high-risk pain situations as well as any core psychological or other coexisting issues such as depression.

Developing an Effective Pain Flare-up Plan

When you live with chronic pain you will probably experience times when your pain levels flare up. Sometimes you can determine why and other times it comes as a complete surprise and you don't really know why. No matter what the reason, your pain flares up; you need to find safe effective ways to cope with the amplified symptoms which requires having a good plan in place. This plan is in addition to your baseline pain management plan—not a replacement of it.

Ongoing pain journaling is one way to be on the lookout for situations or events that trigger your pain flare-ups. You also need to have a variety of tools at your disposal so you can get into quick action to manage your pain flare-ups. I believe that over 90 percent of the time, nonmedication interventions will be the best and most effective. Make sure to discuss this with your pain management doctor.

Below are several nonpharmacological (nonmedication) interventions that other people have learned to implement in order to manage their pain flare-ups. This is followed by a list of alternative interventions for you to choose from. Some of the interventions below may seem similar to the craving management plan—but the focus is different. This plan can actually enhance your craving management plan.

You may already be implementing some of the examples listed below. The important thing to remember is you can always improve your ability to intervene in a way that helps you regain effective pain management. Sometimes the intervention will be pain medication or medical procedures, but changing your medication protocols should only be done with your healthcare provider's knowledge and permission.

- **Relaxation:** When you are in a pain flare-up, your body's automatic response often includes a reflexive tensing response. This problem leads to your being unable to relax the areas of your body where you feel the pain, which leads to increased muscle tension in these areas. You need to practice to consciously relax the affected muscles, enabling them to modulate your pain levels and bring the pain under your control without needing to increase your medication.

- **Increasing Activity/Fitness:** Many people who experience pain flare-ups become very sedentary with strong avoidance tendencies for many types of activities. The two primary reasons for this are the pain itself, and your own predictions regarding the negative impact of the activity. Therefore, it is crucial to return to more normal levels of activities and slowly increase your stamina for physical activities. The goal is to extinguish conditioned avoidance patterns.

- **Diffusing/Reducing Emotional Overreactivity:** When you are experiencing intense uncomfortable emotions, especially about being in pain, your pain levels can actually intensify. Your emotions become like an amplifier circuit that increases the "volume" of your pain. You need to practice specific methods of reducing this automatic process that occurs in the face of stressful triggers. You need to realize that you may not be able to eliminate these problematic emotional triggers, but you can learn different methods of reacting and managing your feelings.
- **External Focusing/Distraction:** The more you focus on your pain, the more you actually intensify your experience of the pain. You need to learn how to shift and manipulate your focus of attention in a positive way, which will minimize your experience of the pain. This can be accomplished by changing how you think and feel about your pain. You can then find pleasant activities or tasks to take your focus off of your pain.
- **Using Anything That Works:** There are numerous interventions that you can attempt when your pain flares up. In addition to those listed above, you can use breathing, muscle relaxation, visual imagery, music, cold/heat, stretching, massage therapy, stress management, acupuncture, acupressure, TENS unit, journaling, and hydrotherapy, to name just a few.

Later in this section you will be asked to make a preliminary list of four or five pain flare-up interventions that you know you can successfully implement the next time you experience a pain flare-up. This is just a starting point. Your plan will need to be modified and improved as you move forward through the remainder of this book and as new ideas come to you. You may want to implement some of the nonpharmacological interventions from the next section.

Nonpharmacological Interventions

Nonpharmacological treatments have proven effective for many pain conditions. For example, recent studies have shown that endorphins mediate the analgesic effects of acupuncture and placebos as well. Still to be discovered is the mechanism by which hypnosis accomplishes its analgesic effects. Some of the nonpharmacological processes are briefly described below.

Meditation and Relaxation

For decades, the addiction treatment (addictive or substance use disorders) research literature has established the effectiveness of teaching meditation and relaxation techniques to people with addiction. The pain literature also indicates the importance of using relaxation to help reduce the level of pain that people living with chronic pain experience. For example in her book, *Managing Pain before it Manages You,* Dr. Margaret Caudill (2008) explains how to evoke what she calls the *relaxation response* in order to reduce stress and pain.

There are many publications available in print or through electronic media that can be used to teach you how to use meditation and relaxation exercises to reduce stress and anxiety. Later you will learn about the stress-pain connection. But remember, in most cases if you can learn to lower your stress level, you will also experience a decrease in your level of pain.

Emotional Management

Most addiction treatment professionals realize the importance of teaching their patients how to appropriately deal with emotional issues to reduce their stress and anxiety. The CENAPS® Model is based in part on the belief that masking or avoiding painful emotions will often lead a recovering chemically dependent person to relapse.

One of the most difficult and crucial, emotional issues that must be resolved is the grief and sense of loss about your health and prior level of functioning. Finding support as you work through a painful grieving process will improve your chances of a successful treatment outcome with chronic pain.

Massage Therapy and Physical Therapy

As we saw earlier, direct pressure can sometimes change the way you experience pain. When using massage therapy you need to understand that there will be some immediate pain relief and reduced muscle tension, but it will be short-lived if not followed with other measures. This is understandable since there are many precursors or triggers for muscle tension that often resurface soon after a massage session. Therefore, other interventions must be implemented that are specific to each individual person, and must be used in the proper sequence.

Many healthcare providers promote the combination of physical therapy and hydrotherapy as you learn how to strengthen and recondition your body, thus becoming an active participant in your healing process.

Chiropractic Treatment

Many chronic pain patients receive long-term pain reduction when undergoing chiropractic treatment. Chiropractic adjustments restore proper motion and function to damaged joints, thereby reducing irritation to associated muscles and nerves.

Most chiropractors are also trained in nutrition and may include dietary changes and nutrient supplementation in their treatment plans. This process helps to build up the immune system while at the same time raising your pain threshold. Some chiropractors are also using *cold laser therapy.*

Acupuncture

Acupuncture is one of the oldest, most commonly used medical procedures in the world. Originating in China more than 2,000 years ago, acupuncture became better known in the United States in 1971, when *New York Times* reporter James Reston wrote about how doctors in China used needles to ease his pain after surgery. The term *acupuncture* describes a family of procedures involving stimulation of anatomical points on the body by a variety of techniques. The acupuncture technique that has been most studied scientifically involves penetrating the skin with thin, solid, metallic needles that are manipulated by the hands or by electrical stimulation.

Acupuncture is often effective in managing certain types of pain. It stimulates the large and small nerve fibers that inhibit pain signaling; and may produce a placebo effect through the release of endorphins and enkephalins (the brain's natural painkillers). Acupuncture is often used in the treatment of back pain, minor surgery, and other pain conditions.

Biofeedback

Biofeedback is a treatment technique where people are trained to improve their health by recognizing and using signals from their own bodies. Physical therapists use biofeedback to help stroke victims regain movement in paralyzed muscles. Psychologists use it to help tense and anxious patients learn to relax. Specialists in many different fields use biofeedback to help their patients cope with pain.

Biofeedback has proven to be another effective method

that you can learn in order to participate more actively in your own treatment. This procedure teaches you how to minimize or eliminate the physical symptoms of stress and tension.

Effective biofeedback treatment is progressive and includes several steps. It starts with an accurate diagnosis of the problem followed by implementation of the appropriate treatment modality specified for you. It also includes time for you to practice situations that simulate instances where the symptoms most often arise. Learning to use meditation and relaxation techniques to reduce stress is also a helpful complement to the biofeedback process.

Hypnosis

Hypnosis can be an effective treatment for various pain conditions. There is some evidence that certain people are more susceptible to the effects of hypnosis than others. The effects of hypnosis are definitely biopsychosocial. Although it is not certain how hypnosis biologically mediates pain, there is growing evidence that it may activate pain-inhibitory descending nerve pathways from brain to spinal cord. It appears, however, that hypnosis does not affect the opioid pathways.

Hypnosis also creates an altered state of consciousness that is usually marked by a slowing of brain wave patterns. As a result, people under the influence of hypnosis often experience a state of consciousness associated with alpha and theta brain wave activity. These states of consciousness bypass normal cognitive processes and hence can prevent many expectations and beliefs about the pain experience (such as, anticipatory pain) from coming to mind.

Psychologically, hypnosis may act in the brain to shift attention away from the pain sensation. Hypnosis is commonly used in conjunction with dental procedures, childbirth, burns, and headaches.

Socially, hypnosis may create a cultural expectation through suggestion that the pain will be minimal and manageable. The social context of hypnotic suggestion may also distract from the pain.

Using the Pain Management Checklist

Below is a checklist of some alternative activities many people living with chronic pain have discovered to be beneficial in more effectively managing their pain. As you read through the list, please check the boxes of those interventions that you have available in your community that you

Pain Management Checklist

☐ Exercise and Stretching	☐ Cognitive Restructuring
☐ Diet/Nutrition	☐ TENS Unit
☐ Physical Therapy	☐ Reflexology
☐ Yoga	☐ PA/AA/NA-type Twelve-Step Meetings
☐ Meditation	☐ Cranial Sacral Therapy
☐ Traditional Native Tribal Healing	☐ Volunteer Work
☐ Talking Circles	☐ Rolfing or Heller Work
☐ Sweat Lodges	☐ Tai Chi or Qigong
☐ Spiritual Retreats	☐ Nature
☐ Faith or Religion	☐ Beach Walks (nature walks)
☐ Prayer	☐ Art Therapy, (collage, pottery)
☐ Sleep Therapy	☐ Camping
☐ Hydrotherapy	☐ Personal Trainer
☐ Healthy Avoidance by Distraction	☐ Sex Therapy
☐ Fishing or Other Hobbies	☐ Chiropractic
☐ Vocational Rehabilitation	☐ EMDR
☐ Acupuncture	☐ Neuro-Linguistic Programming™ (NLP™)
☐ Pet Therapy	☐ Play Therapy
☐ Sandtray Therapy	☐ Hypnosis and Self-Hypnosis
☐ Comedy	☐ Aromatherapy
☐ Family Therapy	☐ Reiki
☐ Biofeedback	☐ Aerobics
☐ Music or Movement Therapy	☐ Humor and/or Comedy

would be able to add to your pain flare-up plan and to your overall pain management program.

Remember the more interventions you add, the better you will be able to manage your pain, and the less likely you will have abuse/addiction problems with your pain medication.

Mary's and Mark's Nonpharmacological Pain Flare-up Plans

Mary's Plan

Taking out her pain journal and writing was the first action Mary committed to taking when she experienced a pain flare-up. She believed this to be the most important step because she could look at the ascending versus descending pain symptoms from the earlier worksheet and see which side was stronger. She did not want to get back into the trap of using medication for her psychological/emotional pain symptoms and she knew this would help her.

Mary did think that it would be challenging, at first—to take this first step—but she was willing to put it on her plan. She believed that by doing the journaling several times a day she would be able to use it for flare-ups and committed to putting it on her plan.

Mary's next plan was to reach out and call one of her support people—either from her church or the Twelve-Step meetings. The first thing she would tell them was that she was having a pain flare-up and needed their support. Mary knew this was going to also be a major challenge for her because she had a pattern of isolation and not sharing with others. Her plan was to share with her support person(s) the results of her journaling and ask them to talk with her to help her stay focused.

The third step of her plan, if the first two weren't successful, was to listen to her *Self-Hypnotic Pain Relief* CD (by

Potentials Unlimited) and repeat it if necessary. She believed this one would be easier to implement since she experienced several incidents of using this CD which brought the levels of her pain down between two to four points on the 0 to 10 pain scale. She also committed to using this CD on a daily basis as it was recommended by the developer and to listen to the "Subliminal" track at least once a day while she was doing other things.

Her final step was to get an appointment for either acupuncture or massage therapy as soon as possible, as well as calling her pain management doctor if the flare-up lasted more than several hours. She knew from past experience that acupuncture and massage helped her break previous pain flare-up cycles and believed she could be very successful adding this to her pain flare-up plan. I encouraged her to be thinking of other interventions she could add on an ongoing basis in order to build a strong toolbox that would always have something she could use to successfully manage her pain flare-ups.

Mark's Plan

Like Mary, Mark also thought using the ascending/descending worksheet would be a great idea. In order to help him be successful using this for pain flare-ups, he committed to using it on a daily basis as part of his pain journaling process. He agreed to bring his daily and weekly journaling assignments to our sessions and gave me permission to help him hold himself accountable to doing this on an ongoing basis.

The next tool Mark committed to use was healthy avoidance by distraction—taking the focus off his "suffering" and placing it on something positive and beneficial. He had learned that when he did certain moving meditation activities such as tai chi, that he was no longer focused on his pain. He also knew from past experience that movement

183

and stretching helped him reduce the severity of his pain symptoms so this was important for him and thus he would be more likely to use this during a pain flare-up.

The third intervention was going back over his depression management and TFUAR exercises and pulling out one of those interventions. The major one he chose was to identify the self-defeating or irrational thoughts, uncomfortable feelings, self-defeating urges, and self-destructive behaviors he tends to exhibit during a pain flare-up and replace them with solution interventions. He believes he can be very successful with this tool because he has his positive past TFUAR exercises and journaling assignment results to draw from.

The final tool Mark chose was to either soak in his hot tub or, if possible, go swimming. He knew from past experience that water was very healing for him. He could also use the opportunity to socialize if he went to the pool to swim or walk in the water. This also helped him achieve his goal of not isolating and sharing with trusted others what was going on for him.

Now It's Your Turn

Take some time right now to imagine yourself in a situation when you are experiencing a pain flare-up and need to intervene in a positive and proactive manner. Below is space to list four of your own nonpharmacological (nonmedication) activities that you are willing to add to your personal pain management program.

You may want to write these out in your own journal at this point. You will also be asked to answer some probing questions and make a personal commitment to succeeding with this new plan. Please remember that the stronger your plan is, the more successful you will be in managing your pain flare-ups.

Your Personal Nonpharmacological Pain Flare-up Plan

1. What is the first activity you chose? _____

   - Why was it important to choose this activity? _____
   _____
   _____

   - What obstacles can you see getting in the way of utilizing this activity? _____
   _____
   _____

   - What is your plan to overcome those obstacles (you may need to ask for help)? _____
   _____
   _____

   - Are you willing to commit to implementing this new pain management activity?
   ❏ Yes ❏ No ❏ Unsure
   Please explain your answer: _____
   _____
   _____
   _____

2. What is the second activity you chose? _____
   - Why was it important to choose this activity? _____
   _____
   _____

   - What obstacles can you see getting in the way of utilizing this activity? _____
   _____
   _____

   - What is your plan to overcome those obstacles (you may need to ask for help)? _____
   _____
   _____

- Are you willing to commit to implementing this new pain management activity?
  ❏ Yes   ❏ No   ❏ Unsure
  Please explain your answer: _____

  _____

  _____

  _____

3. What is the third activity you chose? _____
   - Why was it important to choose this activity? _____

     _____

     _____

   - What obstacles can you see getting in the way of utilizing this activity? _____

     _____

     _____

   - What is your plan to overcome those obstacles (you may need to ask for help)? _____

     _____

     _____

     _____

   - Are you willing to commit to implementing this new pain management activity?
     ❏ Yes   ❏ No   ❏ Unsure
     Please explain your answer: _____

     _____

     _____

     _____

4. What is the fourth activity you chose? _____
   - Why was it important to choose this activity? _____

     _____

     _____

   - What obstacles can you see getting in the way of utilizing this activity? _____

     _____

     _____

- What is your plan to overcome those obstacles (you may need to ask for help)? _____

_____

_____

- Are you willing to commit to implementing this new pain management activity?
  ❏ Yes ❏ No ❏ Unsure
  Please explain your answer: _____

_____

_____

5. What obstacles could stop you from implementing your new four-part plan and what are you willing to commit to do to overcome those obstacles?

- Please list the obstacles and explain how you would overcome them: _____

_____

_____

_____

_____

_____

Your Fourth Step Call to Action

You have now completed the fourth step of your pain management journey and here is your opportunity to summarize your experience in this step. Please answer the three questions below:

1. What is the most important thing you have learned about yourself and your pain management as a result of completing this step?

_____

_____

_____

_____

_____

2. What are you willing to commit to do differently as a result of what you have learned by completing this step?

_____

_____

_____

_____

_____

_____

3. What obstacles might get in the way of your making these changes and what can you do to overcome those roadblocks?

_____

_____

_____

_____

_____

_____

_____

**Please Take Time to
Pause, Rest, and Reflect
Then Go on to Step Five**

Step Five:
To Medicate or Not to Medicate—That *Is* the Question

Beware of the Quick Fix Trap

When you live with chronic pain it can become very frustrating when you aren't getting the pain relief you want. I know that when I experience a pain flare-up my first reaction is I want it to stop—now! Many of the pain medications were developed for acute pain conditions. It can soon become very problematic when you use an acute pain plan on a chronic pain condition. Some people have a need for *instant gratification* (I want it and I want it now). Unfortunately, some of the acute pain medication leads people into this instant gratification trap—looking for the quick fix. This section will help you take a look at your relationship with pain medication.

Telling the difference between appropriate and effective use of pain medication and the beginning of medication abuse can sometimes be difficult for you or your healthcare providers to determine. There are progressive stages of problematic use including medication dependency, medication abuse, pseudoaddiction, and finally addiction. The confusion and uncertainty of this progression is a challenge for both you and your treatment provider.

Some people living with chronic pain are afraid to take their narcotic (opiates, etc.) medication because they have heard horror stories of people getting hooked on pain pills.

This leads to a decision to undermedicate and results in suffering. If you happen to be in recovery for alcoholism or any other drug addiction, the problem is even worse. If you undermedicate it could trigger a relapse. Of course the other side of the coin is overmedication, which could lead to rapid tolerance building and finally reactivation of your addiction.

Your Personal Beliefs about Pain and Medication

Often a decision to use pain medication has been made because a doctor prescribed it; usually after only a very brief consultation. Many doctors have minimal training in addiction and may not be aware of the risks for some of their patients. On the other hand, some people mislead their doctors (intentionally or unintentionally), by not giving them an accurate picture of their past history (or family history) of alcohol or other drug problems. Other factors in medication decision making center on your response to, and beliefs about, pain.

Below is information used with permission from my *Addiction-Free Pain Management® Recovery Guide* on the exercise designed to help people make healthier decisions about pain medication use. The overall purpose of this exercise is for you to explore how you make decisions, so you can begin to make accurate, honest, and healthy choices about your pain management and use of pain medication.

In this exercise you are asked to think back to the very first time you took any medication (including alcohol) for pain relief and write about it like a story with a beginning, middle, and end. Make sure to include: your age at the time, what you were doing, who you were with, what happened, what thoughts you had about your pain, how you were affected (or what feelings were produced) by the pain, who suggested the pain medication, what it was, and how much you used.

You are then asked what you wanted the medication to do for you and what you wanted the medication to help you cope with or escape from. See the following table for the questions asked in this exercise. Please take a few moments to record your answers in your journal.

Your Personal Beliefs About Pain and Medication

1. Think back to the very first time you took any medication (including alcohol) for pain relief and write it like a story with a beginning, middle, and end. Make sure to include your age at the time, what you were doing, who you were with, what happened, what you were thinking about your pain, how you were affected (or feelings produced) by the pain, who suggested the pain medication, what it was, and how much you used.
2. What did you want the medication to do for you?
3. What did you want the medication to help you cope with or escape from?
4. What happened when you were growing up in your family when someone was in pain? What were the messages you received about pain and pain management?
5. What's the most important thing you learned from completing this part of the exercise and what can you do differently for your pain management as a result?

Defining Misunderstood Terms

There is quite a bit of confusion and mislabeling of people on long-term use of pain medication. Many patients are identified as "addicts" when they really are not. To help clarify this issue a consensus document was developed by the American Academy of Pain Medicine, the American Pain Society, and the American Society of Addiction. They have agreed upon the following definitions for *tolerance, physical dependence, pseudoaddiction,* and *addiction*:

Tolerance

Tolerance is a state of adaptation in which exposure to a drug induces changes that result in a diminution of one or more of the drug's effects over time. To put it simply, tolerance means that it takes more medication to get the same level of pain relief.

Physical Dependence

Physical dependence is a state of adaptation that is manifested by a drug class specific withdrawal syndrome that can be produced by abrupt cessation, rapid dose reduction, decreasing blood level of the drug, and/or administration of an antagonist.

Pseudoaddiction

The term pseudoaddiction has developed over the past several years in an attempt to explain and understand how some chronic pain patients exhibit many red flags that look like addiction. Pseudoaddiction is a term which has been used to describe patient behaviors that may occur when pain is undertreated. Patients with unrelieved pain may become focused on obtaining medications, may clock-watch, and may otherwise seem inappropriately drug seeking. Even such behaviors as illicit drug use and deception can occur in the patient's efforts to obtain relief. Pseudoaddiction can be distinguished from true addiction in that the behaviors resolve when pain is effectively treated.

Addiction

Addiction is a primary, chronic, neurobiological disease, with genetic, psychosocial, and environmental factors influencing its development and manifestations. It is characterized by behaviors that include one or more of the following: impaired control over drug use, compulsive use, continued use despite harm, and craving.

Pseudotolerance

Dr. William W. Deardorff (2004) advocates the importance of differentiating tolerance (described previously) and pseudotolerance. He describes pseudotolerance as the need to increase dosage that is not due to tolerance but due to other factors such as changes in the disease, inadequate pain relief, change in other medication, increased physical activity, drug interactions, lack of compliance, etc. Examples of pseudotolerance in a patient's behavior may include drug seeking, clock-watching for dosing, and even illicit drug use in an effort to obtain relief. Like pseudoaddiction, pseudotolerance can be distinguished from addiction in that the behaviors resolve once the pain is effectively treated.

Physical Dependency versus Addiction

Not everyone who uses pain medication on an ongoing basis will become addicted. You may in fact become physically dependent to the medication, but may not experience pseudoaddiction, pseudotolerance, or addiction.

It's Important to Understand Addiction

In this section I want to expand upon the definition used earlier. Here I use the terms *addictive disorders* and *addiction* to discuss what the DSM-IV-TR™ (*Diagnostic and Statistical Manual of Mental Disorders; Fourth Edition, Text Revision*) classifies as *substance use disorders* and is also referred to as *chemical dependency,* or *psychological dependence*.

Here I define addictive disorder as: A collection of symptoms (i.e., a syndrome) that is caused by a pathological response to the ingestion of mood-altering substances and has ten major characteristics. These characteristics are listed in the following table.

Common Addictive Disorder Symptoms

1. Euphoria	6. Inability to Abstain
2. Craving	7. Addiction-Centered Lifestyle
3. Tolerance	8. Addictive Lifestyle Losses
4. Loss of Control	9. Continued Use Despite Problems
5. Withdrawal	10. Substance-Induced Organic Mental Disorders

Differentiating Between Addiction and Pseudoaddiction

No one undergoing chronic pain management starts out with the goal of becoming addicted to their pain medication; nevertheless it happens at least 10 percent of the time. If someone has a family history of addiction or mental health conditions, or if they have a personal history of addiction or mental health problems, they have a higher risk of racing through the progression of addiction.

People at risk for addiction react differently from the very first experience of taking pain medication. With ongoing exposure they experience the "seeking reaching" stage, at which time doctor shopping can begin. There are many questions to be addressed when treating someone who has chronic pain and coexisting substance use disorders. The three most important ones I talk about at my Addiction-Free Pain Management® trainings are these:

1. Are we managing pain but fueling the addiction?
2. Are we treating the addiction but sabotaging the pain management?
3. Is it addiction or pseudoaddiction?

The term pseudoaddiction is fairly new to the addiction treatment field but has been used in pain management for quite a while now. The point to remember is that even though pseudoaddiction looks like addiction, it is actually caused by an undertreated or mistreated chronic pain condition. However, the treatment plan for pseudoaddiction and addiction is identical. The major danger of pseudoaddiction is that if it is not *adequately* addressed, it will turn into full blown addiction—sometimes quickly, sometimes slowly.

I have worked with many patients over the years who were labeled prescription drug addicts when the correct diagnosis was pseudoaddiction. One patient, Sharon, is an example of how damaging a misdiagnosis can be. Sharon was in her early forties and came from a fairly normal and religious upbringing. She had never used alcohol or any other drugs, including nicotine, and up until a few years ago had never used psychoactive prescription medications either.

A few years before I started working with Sharon she began having infrequent migraine headaches. She went to her general practitioner and was given Vicodin to help with the pain which worked for a time. Sharon later found out that she would have been better off using migraine specific medication. As the Vicodin began losing its effectiveness her doctor prescribed OxyContin but she also used Vicodin for *breakthrough pain.*

Although barbiturates and opioids are sometimes considered effective for short-term migraine relief, many doctors are now recommending against prescribing this type of medication for long-term use. The risks for potential dependence and abuse are too high and there is a real danger of developing medication overuse headaches (sometimes called *pain rebound* or *transformed migraines*).

Because transformed migraines are difficult to diagnose, many people are not being treated appropriately. Treatment is further complicated by the chronic nature of migraine headaches. People with transformed migraines may overuse pain relievers, both prescription and over-the-counter, on a daily basis with or without having a headache. This puts them at risk for building a tolerance to the drugs. Additionally, taking too many pain relievers containing caffeine can also lead to rebound headaches.

Sharon's migraines became more frequent and she had to take more and more medication to get any relief. As the dose increased, her family and then her doctor became concerned that she had become "addicted" to the OxyContin and Vicodin. Sharon's doctor told her he couldn't help her anymore unless she went into an addiction treatment program. Her family found an addiction treatment program that said they treated pain and prescription drug addiction.

This is when Sharon's nightmare began. While undergoing detoxification from the OxyContin and Vicodin, Sharon was forced to stand up in front of groups and identify herself as a drug addict. She was not even allowed to say she was a prescription drug addict, which was humiliating for this very conservative woman.

After Sharon stopped all of her medications, the migraines kept coming back. To add insult to injury, when she asked for help with the migraines the program staff said she was "drug seeking" and all she needed to do was "turn it over" and work the steps. Even though I'm a big advocate of a Twelve-Step approach for people with addictive disorders, it can be dangerous to label or advise chronic pain patients.

Sharon was discharged from this program with a letter to her doctor stating she was an addict and should not be given opiates anymore. When she became depressed and attempted suicide her family was able to send Sharon to the pain clinic where I was consulting. I met with Sharon several times, assessed her case and discovered that her diagnosis was not addiction; but pseudoaddiction.

As mentioned above, pseudoaddiction describes patient behaviors that may occur when pain is undertreated. People with unrelieved pain may become focused on obtaining medications, clock-watch, or otherwise seem to be inappropriately drug seeking. Even such behaviors as illicit drug use and deception can occur in the person's efforts to obtain relief. Pseudoaddiction can be distinguished from true addiction in that the behaviors will resolve when the pain is effectively treated.

Addiction versus Pseudoaddiction

- Pseudoaddiction looks a lot like addiction
- Patients may appear to be "drug seeking"
- Patients may need frequent early refills
- Behaviors are caused by undertreatment
- Problematic behaviors resolve when the patient's pain is adequately treated

This was the case for Sharon. The pain clinic decided to use migraine specific medications since opiates are contraindicated for ongoing migraine treatment. There are seven *triptans* (Imitrex, Maxalt, Zomig, Amerge, Axert, Frova, and Relpax) that were developed for and FDA approved as migraine abortive (management) medications. These medications work to stop the migrainous process in the brain and stop an attack with its associated symptoms.

Sharon responded well to Maxalt, but she also was put on a preventative medication. *Ergotamine* medications, such as dihydroergotamine (DHE) and Migranal, are used as vasoconstrictors for migraine prevention and sometimes mixed with caffeine. They are also FDA approved for migraine treatment as is Midrin (a combination of acetaminophen, dichloralphenazone, and isometheptene). Sharon was also prescribed Migranal. Because of these two medications, her migraines were now being effectively managed.

Sharon was also prescribed a selective serotonin reuptake inhibitor (SSRI) antidepressant as I implemented a cognitive-behavioral therapy treatment plan for the depression and pain-focused psychotherapy for pain management. Today Sharon is once again experiencing a great quality of life, but still has nightmares about her time at the treatment program. Getting back to my original three questions; Sharon's general practitioner was at risk of fueling addiction and the addiction treatment program definitely sabotaged her pain management.

It is important to obtain multidisciplinary assessments and be open to discovering whether you are experiencing addiction or pseudoaddiction if you experience chronic pain and coexisting addictive disorders. Sharon experienced pseudoaddiction—not addiction as everyone thought. Once Sharon was placed on an appropriate migraine medication management plan, along with cognitive-behavioral therapy to address the psychological pain symptoms, her quality of life improved dramatically and her migraine episodes lessened both in frequency and intensity.

Understanding and Treating the Addiction Pain Syndrome™

Pain is the reason many people start using potentially addictive substances. Jeanie is an excellent example of what can happen when a pain condition is not managed appropriately and treatment depends only on medication.

We know that regular use of psychoactive medication plus a genetic or environmental susceptibility can lead from pain relief to increased tolerance. Both of Jeanie's parents were alcoholics and she was in an abusive marriage. She then developed a chronic pain condition and was prescribed opiate medication to treat her pain. Jeanie soon discovered that her pain medication also helped her escape from painful childhood memories and the trauma of an abusive relationship.

Eventually Jeanie's medication no longer helped her physical pain symptoms or emotional distress, so she started taking much more than was prescribed. She eventually went to several different doctors to get the amount she believed she needed, but her pain continued to get worse. In fact, Jeanie's medication actually started increasing or amplifying her pain signals—this is called the *pain rebound effect.*

The end result for Jeanie was an addiction to her medication that increased her pain and created problems in every area of her life; physically, psychologically, and socially (biopsychosocial). Because Jeanie was experiencing both chronic pain and substance dependency problems, she needed a specialized concurrent treatment plan for both conditions.

Physical pain is the reason many people like Jeanie start using potentially addictive substances. Chronic medication use plus genetic or environmental susceptibility can lead to increased tolerance as a result of searching for pain relief. Eventually the addictive substance no longer manages the pain symptoms. In fact, it often increases or amplifies the pain signals—a condition called hyperalgesia (an extreme sensitivity to pain) can also develop. The end result is severe biopsychosocial pain and problems.

In 1996, I conducted research to begin developing the first clinical skills training for Addiction-Free Pain Management®. What I looked for was information on people who had chronic pain and coexisting addiction. I was disturbed to discover there was no information. What I did find was an abundance of information on people with addiction and quite a bit about people who had chronic pain. But I couldn't find anything that addressed someone who suffered with both conditions. As a result I developed the Addiction Pain Syndrome™ which is described below.

Since I couldn't find any research, I started conducting my own and discovered that historically, pain conditions and addictive disorders have been treated as separate issues.

Pain clinics have had great success in treating chronic pain conditions. Addiction treatment programs have had success in treating addictive disorders. However, both modalities often struggle when the patient is suffering from both conditions.

As you can see from the Addiction Pain Syndrome™ diagram shown below, addiction treatment programs cover about a third of the problem (the *Addictive Disorder Zone*) when dealing with a chronic pain patient. The pain clinics cover a different third of the problem (the *Pain Disorder Zone*). Each of the above modalities when implemented independently misses about two-thirds of the problem.

Sometimes addiction treatment centers recognize the need to refer a patient to a pain specialist or the pain clinics refer a patient to an addiction specialist. This is definitely an improvement. Now about two-thirds of the patient's needs are being addressed (both the Addictive Disorder Zone and the Pain Disorder Zone). But what about the third zone?

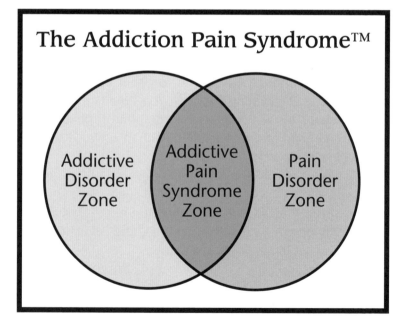

The Addiction Pain Syndrome™

Addictive Disorder Zone

Addictive Pain Syndrome Zone

Pain Disorder Zone

The center area in the diagram is the *Addiction Pain Syndrome Zone*. This is why I developed the Addiction-Free Pain Management® (APM) System.

APM™ concurrently addresses the addictive disorder, the pain disorder, and the addiction pain syndrome. All three zones are addressed—the Addictive Disorder Zone, the Pain Disorder Zone, and the Addiction Pain Syndrome Zone.

The negative consequences more than double when patients experience both addictive disorders and pain disorders. Addictive disorders lead to one universe of biopsychosocial problems, and the pain disorders lead to a different set of problems. 1 + 1 no longer equals 2, rather 1 + 1 now equals 3 or more. This is called *synergism*. Synergism is a condition where the combined action is greater in total effect than the sum of the individual effects.

Synergistic Symptoms

Take another look at the Addiction Pain Syndrome™ diagram, and notice the area labeled the *Addictive Disorder Zone*. Now look at the *Pain Disorder Zone*. When these two zones are added together, we have the sum of both zones plus a new zone—the *Addiction Pain Syndrome Zone*. A new universe of symptoms occurs due to the synergistic effect.

When Jeanie's negative consequences from the Addictive Disorder Zone and her Pain Disorder Zone were added together she experienced not only the problems of both zones but also additional problems from the Addiction Pain Syndrome Zone. Her synergistic symptoms occurred due to the combined effect. To have successful treatment outcomes this phenomenon must be addressed through a specialized treatment approach—a *synergistic treatment system*. The Addiction-Free Pain Management® (APM) System is such a treatment system. APM™ addresses the addictive disorder, the pain disorder, and the addiction pain syndrome.

An effective synergistic treatment protocol for Jeanie's

chronic pain and substance dependency issues needed to include the three following components we covered earlier:

- Appropriate Medication Management
- Core Clinical Processes
- Nonpharmacological Interventions

1. **Appropriate Medication Management:** For this component to be effective it is important to find a doctor that is addiction medicine certified—a call to a local drug treatment program may be necessary to find this person. Jeanie's medication management plan included collaborating with an addiction medicine practitioner/specialist to make sure that her medication was needed, was recovery friendly and was the right type, as well as the appropriate quantity and frequency, so it would not trigger relapse or end up with Jeanie abusing her medication again.

2. **Core Clinical Processes:** Jeanie also needed to deal with her irrational thinking, uncomfortable emotions, and self-defeating urges and behaviors as well as the isolation tendencies that come about with pain and addiction. This required a cognitive-behavioral therapy approach using the eight clinical processes in the *Addiction-Free Pain Management® Workbook* as a starting point. This process worked well for Jeanie because her healthcare provider was experienced in the concurrent treatment of chronic pain and substance dependency.

3. **Nonpharmacological (Nonmedication) Interventions:** This process included Jeanie searching out alternative nonpharmacological/holistic pain management modalities such as hydrotherapy, physical therapy, acupuncture, chiropractic, prayer, meditation, self-hypnosis, and hypnosis. Also, reading *Managing Pain Before it Manages You*

(2001), a book by Margaret Caudill, was very helpful for Jeanie. Jeanie also got connected with both a Twelve-Step group and a chronic pain support group, which greatly enhanced her recovery.

Developing an effective treatment plan also required knowing which stage of the problem Jeanie was in. It was important for her to know how much damage had been done by her inappropriate use of pain medication and which stage of the addiction process she was at. As Jeanie moved into recovery it was also essential to understand which stage of the developmental recovery process she was in so she could implement appropriate treatment interventions.

As you can see, the road to recovery is a difficult one for someone with both chronic pain and a coexisting addictive disorder. However, most of the chronic pain research I have reviewed over the past two decades has been very clear about treatment outcomes. The best prognosis is when people are proactive in their own treatment and recovery process. One way they can do this is to learn as much about their pain and effective pain management as they can.

As mentioned before, knowledge is power. Once people know what is really going on with their body and mind they can start to take action to effectively manage their pain. In fact, they need to stop seeing pain as their enemy and see it as their friend. I know this is much easier said than done.

Jeanie had a difficult time hearing that she must make peace with her pain, and in fact that pain is her friend. She even told me she didn't believe it, but nevertheless it is true. It was very important for Jeanie to shift from victim mode and empower herself by developing a pain management and chemical dependency recovery program. Fortunately, Jeanie adhered to her treatment plan and remains clean and sober, and is effectively managing her chronic pain.

Learn to Identify Red Flags to Make Healthier Pain Medication Decisions

The following information can help you take a look at your relationship with pain medication. Differentiating between appropriate use of pain medication and the beginning of abuse can be difficult to determine. Remember, there are progressive stages of problematic use including medication dependency, medication abuse, pseudoaddiction, and finally addiction.

As mentioned earlier, many people in chronic pain are afraid to take their opiate pain medication because they fear addiction. When they have this fear they tend to undermedicate and then they end up suffering as a result. However, it is necessary to be cautious and have an effective medication management plan in place to avoid potential problems, including abuse or addiction.

If you happen to be in recovery for alcoholism or another drug addiction and you undermedicate, it could trigger a relapse. Overmedication could lead to tolerance building and reactivation of an existing addictive disorder that was in remission.

Looking for Red Flags: Overmedicating and Undermedicating

In the following exercise you will see a list of *red flags* or indicators that someone is using their pain medication in a manner that could eventually lead to problems or even addiction. Both you, your support network, and your treatment providers need to be familiar with these red flags and, if needed, seek professional help from a person trained in addiction who also has experience, understanding, or training in pain management if problems surface.

By doing this you will be able to work with your health-care providers to make better decisions about using potentially problematic pain medication. Before you complete your red flags worksheet first read what Mary and Mark discovered by completing this exercise.

Mary's and Mark's Red Flags Results

Mary's Red Flags Results

This was a very difficult exercise for Mary. She had 13 level 10 answers and several other answers were higher than level 5. After she completed this exercise and reviewed her answers in our session she was ready to admit she had a substance abuse problem. I determined that Mary was probably experiencing pseudoaddiction and not addiction after further assessments and collaboration with her other healthcare providers, as well as noting that the problem behaviors stopped as she managed her pain and depression more effectively.

At this point Mary really was physically and psychologically dependent upon her medication (and alcohol) but it was a direct result of mismanaged chronic pain and untreated depression. Mary's condition stabilized as we continued to work on her depression management and implementing several of the steps you'll see in a later section. She was very grateful for this exercise because it was her turning point in coming out of denial and hopelessness and moving into accepting that she needed to learn how to manage her pain in a safer—and more effective—manner. At this point she started to have hope.

Mark's Red Flags Results

This was not a very difficult exercise for Mark. Although he knew he was having troubles following an effective medication management plan, he didn't realize how often he deviated from the plan. He had 10 level 10 answers and several other answers were between 5 and 8. After he completed this exercise and reviewed his answers in our session he was relieved and fully understood that he had a serious substance abuse problem. After further assessments and collaboration with his other healthcare providers, as well as noting the cravings and urges to abuse, I determined Mark was probably experiencing early-stage addiction. His medication was still strong after he managed his pain and depression more effectively.

At this point Mark also admitted that he really was physically and psychologically dependent upon his medication and wanted help. Like Mary, Mark's condition also stabilized as we continued to work on his depression management and implementing several of the steps you'll see in a later section. He was very open to working on the addiction issues as well as his depression and pain management. At this point he also started to have more hope.

Your Red Flags for Pain Medication Abuse/Addiction

Below is a list of *red flags* or indicators that you might be using your pain medication in a manner that could eventually lead to serious problems or even addiction. Both you and your treatment provider need to be familiar with these red flags and to seek professional help from a person trained in addiction who also has experience, understanding, or training in pain management.

Instructions: Please review each of the following items and rate each on a 0 to 10 scale with 0 meaning this item is not and has not been a problem for me; to 10 meaning this has been or is a serious problem for me.

_____ 1. You still experience a sense of euphoria after adjusting to your medication.

_____ 2. You start to have a preoccupation with your pain medication.

_____ 3. You have urges or cravings to overuse your pain medication.

_____ 4. You experience an abnormal increase in tolerance requiring frequent increases in dose.

_____ 5. You decrease, or refuse to participate in, nonpharmacological pain management activities.

_____ 6. You are using non-prescribed substances including alcohol and/or other drugs such as, marijuana, over-the-counter analgesics, and methamphetamine.

_____ 7. You are unable to take your pain medication as prescribed—type, quantity, and/or frequency.

_____ 8. You are experiencing problems with cognition, affect, and/or behavior.

_____ 9. Your quality of life and/or relationships are being negatively impacted by your use of pain medication.

_____ 10. You continue problematic use of medication despite negative consequences.

_____ 11. You use medications in physically dangerous situations, for example, driving a car, operating power tools, or providing childcare to young children.

_____ 12. You experience withdrawal symptoms if you go too long between doses or stop your medication abruptly.

_____ 13. You are experiencing medication-related legal problems; such as, diverting, forgery, doctor shopping, and emergency room hopping.

_____ 14. You are not informing one healthcare provider what medication another provider is prescribing.

_____ 15. You have a history—or family history—of alcoholism or other drug addiction.

_____ 16. You are using the medication to cope with psychological/emotional type pain or to cope with stressful or uncomfortable situations.

_____ 17. Family members or friends report concerns about your use of medication.

_____ 18. You believe you are having problems with your medication.

_____ 19. You are unable to fulfill major obligations with family, friends, and/or work due to your use of medication.

_____ 20. You frequently need early refills and may rationalize this by coming up with sometimes unusual excuses: I lost it, someone else took it, it fell in the water, etc.

_____ 21. You are resistant to referrals for psychological assessment and/or treatment.

_____ 22. You are resistant to non-narcotic medications or referrals for nonmedication type pain management interventions or make excuses why they won't work.

_____ 23. You are resistant to sign consent to release forms allowing your provider to discuss your treatment with other healthcare providers you have been seeing.

_____ 24. You are more concerned about the medication than your pain condition.

_____ 25. You report multiple medication allergies/sensitivities, say you cannot take generic medications or have an extremely sophisticated knowledge of medications.

What Your Answers Mean

Some of the items above may be difficult to determine, which is why collaboration is so essential. This collaboration should include the patient, the patient's support network, other healthcare providers, or any other sources that could help validate the needed information. It is time for a referral to an appropriate addiction specialist to make a more accurate assessment of a potential medication abuse/addiction problem if several of the red flag areas have scores above a 5, or a few have scores in the 8–10 range.

The Obstacle Called Denial

It might be helpful for you to go back to step one and go over the information on denial and review the *Denial Pattern Checklist*. As you learned in step one, a major obstacle to recognizing any problem, including these red flags, and achieving effective pain treatment is the denial system—the psychological defense mechanism that is there to protect you from unbearable situations. It is important to remember that you developed this defense system to protect you from being overwhelmed by what I call *painful reality.*

There are times when this defense mechanism of denial can help. Unfortunately, it can sometimes lead you to avoid looking at and dealing with a situation that is causing life-damaging consequences. There is also another interesting point about denial. If you are told "you're in denial" you are now in a no-win position. If you are in denial you don't know it, and if you're not in denial you can't prove it to the satisfaction of your accuser.

After completing the red flags exercise and looking at possible defense or denial patterns it is time to make a decision. Is it possible that you may need to change your relationship with your pain management medication? What are you willing to do if you have discovered that you experienced some—or many—of the red flags and can see that you may have been caught unaware that a medication management problem was occurring?

Making an Agreement for Success

If you answered "yes" about needing a change, you may want to develop the type of pain medication agreement that I use with most of my patients, especially those who have a history of having problems with misuse/abuse of their pain medications. Remember that this is something you will want to share with your pain management team. They may even have their own medication agreements or contracts that they will expect you to adhere to while under their medical care.

Again, it is important to keep in mind that there are two primary reasons for completing this type of an agreement. The first is for your protection, to make sure you know what is expected of you. The second is to help your provider demonstrate that you both are taking precautions to reduce potential negative consequences while taking your pain medication(s).

In the table below is a sample of a pain management medication agreement I use.

Pain Management Medication Agreement

I,_____, do hereby agree to ABSTAIN from using any *inappropriate* pain medication (*including alcohol*) or any other mood-altering drugs and to continue an effective pain management program while I am working with _____
(your pain management doctor/therapist). Inappropriate medication is anything not approved by

_____

(your pain management doctor/therapist) and includes not taking any medication prescribed for anyone else. Appropriate medication is limited to prescriptions from a provider agreed upon by myself and

_____

(your pain management doctor/therapist) as well as any approved over-the-counter medications jointly agreed upon.

I also agree to submit to random drug screens at the discretion of _____
(your pain management doctor/therapist). Unwillingness to submit to testing will be interpreted as a clear indicator that I have been using mood-altering chemicals or drinking alcohol and that I need immediate intervention.

Should I start using any inappropriate pain medication (*including alcohol*) or other mood-altering drugs and/or deviating from my pain management program, I will immediately seek help from

_____

(your pain management doctor/therapist). I will also be open to outpatient or residential inpatient treatment if determined necessary by

_____

(your pain management doctor/therapist).
　Failure to comply with_____
(your pain management doctor/therapist) recommended interventions is a decision that I no longer wish to receive treatment from

_____

(your pain management doctor/therapist).
　I will consult with _____
(your pain management doctor/therapist) regarding any medications to be prescribed for me by any other physician not previously authorized. His/her phone number is:

_____

_____	_____
Patient Signature	Date
_____	_____
Signature of Witness	Date

Your Fifth Step Call to Action

You have now completed the fifth step of your pain management journey and here is your opportunity to summarize your experience in this step. Please answer the three questions below:

1. What is the most important thing you have learned about yourself and your pain management as a result of completing this step?

   _____

   _____

   _____

   _____

2. What are you willing to commit to do differently as a result of what you have learned by completing this step?

   _____

   _____

   _____

   _____

3. What obstacles might get in the way of your making these changes and what can you do to overcome those roadblocks?

   _____

   _____

   _____

   _____

**Please Take Time to
Pause, Rest, and Reflect
Then Go on to Step Six**

Step Six:
Overcoming the Five Stuck Points to Achieving Full Freedom

You have now covered the first five of the seven essential steps on your journey to freedom from suffering. In this step you will learn the healing process has identifiable stages that move someone from suffering with their pain to thriving and enjoying a wonderful quality of life. Unfortunately, there are no shortcuts and you must be willing and motivated to do the work.

Like in the life process, in pain management there are natural transitions from one stage to the next on your journey. There are also transitions within each of the seven steps of your journey. Unfortunately, there are also five areas where you can get trapped and stalled—stuck points. You need to learn how to resolve these stuck points in order to obtain full freedom from suffering.

The better you get at identifying and traversing those stuck points, the smoother your journey will be. Setting and navigating your course is important as you move toward the final leg of your pain management journey. As I mentioned several times before, knowledge is power; however, knowledge and insight without action will not lead to freedom—you need to do the footwork.

> A little knowledge that acts is worth infinitely more than much knowledge that is idle.—Kahlil Gibran

The Healing Continuum

In the healing continuum diagram below, you see the seven steps to freedom laid out in a linear fashion. Unfortunately, the healing journey is not often that direct. Sometimes the process is three steps forward and one back. At other times it might be one step forward and three back. The important thing to remember is you can do this if you are willing to follow the road map and recognize the roadblocks along the way. It requires action to overcome these obstacles.

There are developmental challenges to overcome in each step of this journey. In this step you are invited to look back at the journey so far and notice what stuck points or areas need improvement before moving to the final step in this journey. As you'll learn in the next step, however, the journey is just beginning and will continue the rest of your life.

Identifying and Managing the Five Stuck Points

It's very important to recognize your stuck points in any phase of the healing continuum. Over the years I've seen many of my patients stop when they are not able to make successful transitions in one or more of the five areas listed below.

- Hopeless to Hopeful
- Demoralized to Revitalized
- Victim to Victorious
- Powerless to Empowered
- Surviving to Thriving

In the following five sections you will see the problem side of each transition point and the importance of moving into the solution. Some of you may see where you have been or are currently stuck and where you need to move forward—or as I tell my patients "Onward and Upward!"

One important point to remember is that this process is different for each person. Some people never experience any of these stuck points while others hit them all. Some of you may hit one or two or even three or four of these obstacles to freedom. That is why it is so important to understand these potential roadblocks and more importantly that once you identify being stuck in any one of them, you can then choose to take action to move out of the problem and into the healthy solution.

Stuck Point One: Hopeless to Hopeful

Have you ever felt hopeless and helpless regarding living with chronic pain? If so, take yourself back to a time when you were the most fearful, overwhelmed, or felt hopeless. Remember how living in that state of mind seemed to drain all of your energy and hope for your future. One of my patients, Sheena, had a workplace accident and broke several bones. In addition, she discovered over a year later that she also had severe nerve damage.

Her doctors tried various pain medications and physical therapy interventions in her first year while she kept trying to return to her job as a carpenter. Unfortunately, each time she tried she ended up in so much pain she had to stop working again. She was finally put on total disability and told she would have to learn to live with the pain. Unfortunately, they did not explain to her how she could do that and still have a functional and satisfactory quality of life.

She was finally referred to a pain clinic that I was consulting with. I worked with her and her doctors to find out why nothing so far had helped her pain. As I assessed her pain symptoms I noticed that seven of twenty of her identified pain symptoms were neuropathic. I also discovered that she had never had an MRI for her back. When she was finally referred for an MRI, the results showed significant nerve impingements and damage.

Just learning what was really going on was the start of her transition from hopeless to having renewed hope for her future. Within six months she had adequate pain relief and was undergoing vocational rehabilitation in computer programming. She was very excited about her future. Without this healthy transition, she would have been at high risk for moving into the next stuck point of demoralization.

Stuck Point Two: Demoralized to Revitalized

When you get to the point of demoralization you could be at risk of wanting to quit or give up. At this point some people sink into the pit of depression, may become suicidal or even attempt to kill themselves. This is what happened to Jim, another of my former patients.

Jim had been on total disability for over seven years when I first met him. He was referred to me after completing a mandated stay at a psychiatric hospital for an attempted suicide. At this point he was heavily medicated with anti-depressants and other mood-stabilizing psychiatric medications. His depression was still moderate to severe and he reported pain levels of 9–10 on the 0 to 10 pain scale on bad days and only 7–8 on his best days even with his pain medication.

Our first step was to have him meet with a pain management colleague of mine and start on medication that would address both the depression and his pain symptoms. The doctor chose Cymbalta due to Jim's significant neuropathic pain symptoms. I helped Jim develop a cognitive-behavioral plan and within a few months Jim made the transition from demoralized to revitalized. He felt like he had his life back.

When people stay in the demoralized state during the next stage they can move to the victim stage. In this stage people tend to really alienate or burn out friends and family. They are also at high risk for going into hopelessness yet again.

Stuck Point Three: Victim to Victorious

People who get stuck in this stage start behaving like a victim and are treated like a victim by others. Many people in this stage blame everyone else for their condition and use that as an excuse not to change. When they are in this stage they use a combination of two of the denial patterns discussed earlier—blaming and strategic hopelessness (also known as *diagnosing myself as beyond help*). Another patient of mine, Shelly, is a prime example of this stuck point.

When I first met Shelly she was hopeless, demoralized,

and felt like a victim. Shelly was a medical doctor who was eventually arrested for diverting medications from her hospital and put in the physician diversion program. She was at high risk for having her license to practice medicine revoked. She started out self-medicating a back pain condition; she eventually became addicted to her medication and began forging prescriptions, then stealing medications from the hospital where she worked.

She was also angry about being in diversion and it was always everybody else's fault. When told she would be drug tested and could no longer take any psychoactive (mood-altering) medications she became depressed and hopeless. In addition to the two denial patterns mentioned above she also used the one about comparison—"I can't be an addict because I take prescription medication for my legitimate pain and I'm a doctor."

The reality is many doctors do become addicted to medications. There is a dangerous mistaken belief in the healthcare community that if you have real pain you will not become addicted. This might be true for most people but 10 to 15 percent of the population can experience medication abuse, pseudoaddiction, or addiction. Fortunately for Shelly, she finally accepted that she had an addictive disorder and that she did it to herself. She now realized she could be victorious and successfully complete her diversion program and go back to the job she loved.

Before moving into the victorious stage Shelly did hit the roadblock of feeling totally powerless. The paradox for her was she had to admit she was powerless over her addiction before she could move into recovery and become victorious.

Stuck Point Four: Powerless to Empowered

Some people are not that fortunate; when they hit the powerless stage they can quickly move to demoralized and hopeless. When these people feel powerless, they give up and sometimes can become so depressed they become suicidal. One tool I teach my patients is the "Serenity Prayer"— made popular by Alcoholics Anonymous (AA)—that I've included here.

> God grant me the serenity to accept the things I cannot change; the courage to change the things I can; and the wisdom to know the difference. —Reinhold Niebuhr

For some of my patients I reframe this as the "Courage Prayer" and help them focus on the courage to change the things they can. For example, Shelly had to accept that she really did have an addictive disorder. Her next step was even more important. She had to be courageous enough to admit that she had a problem and then get into immediate action to get out of the problem and into the solution.

As covered in an earlier chapter, there is a difference between pain and suffering. When people hit this powerless stage I remind them they are powerless over the ascending pain signals, but suffering is a choice. They don't have to suffer if they are courageous enough to do what it takes to more effectively manage their pain and make friends with it. They do have great deal of influence over their descending pain signals.

Once into acceptance, empowerment can quickly follow. When people feel empowered they are more likely to do whatever it takes for effective pain management and to achieve an improved quality of life. At this point some people start to believe they really will be able to survive their pain condition. Getting to this point is important, but if they stay at this stage they will never realize true freedom.

Stuck Point Five: Surviving to Thriving

When people get to this stage I remind them the journey is not yet over; if they stop here they will miss so much.

It's like climbing Mount Everest and getting to the last base camp then stopping when the summit is only one more day away.

On my personal journey, thriving was also the last stage of a grieving process I needed to work through. I had always believed that acceptance was the last stage of the grieving process. I learned that there is another step—reintegration. For me that means I can honestly say that today my life is better than ever—yes, it's different—but I'm living a life with great purpose and meaning even though I am living and thriving with chronic pain.

As I mentioned in my introduction, I almost got stuck in the hopeless and demoralized stage. This is where I even considered suicide as a viable option. But as I was going through the vocational rehabilitation process, I finally got to the point where I could accept what had happened to me and I decided to go on.

Part of my vocational rehabilitation included going back to school to become a counselor which required personal therapy. Lynn Wiese, my therapist for many years, helped me work through the last stages of my grieving process for my lost level of functioning and quality of life.

One of my biggest breakthroughs was getting to the point where I could go and watch my former dojo mates compete in a major karate tournament. I went through a gamut of emotions and almost ran out several times, but I did persevere and stay until the end. From that point on I quit looking back and focused on what I wanted my future to look like instead of focusing on suffering, on what I lost, and what I didn't like.

An important part of moving from surviving to thriving is making friends with pain instead of fighting it all the time or being afraid of it. Sometimes I help my patients with this transition from enemy to friend through art work. I still remember one of my patients from 1996. Sue was really into suffering with her pain, feeling victimized by it, and feeling let down by the healthcare system.

To help Sue with her transition, I asked her to create an artistic interpretation of her pain at its worst. She came to our next session with a drawing of a very ferocious and frightening dragon. The colors she chose were black and blood red. The dragon had fire coming out of its mouth. It had large sharp fangs and claws.

As we got close to completion of our treatment process, I asked Sue to make a new artistic interpretation of her relationship with her pain. She brought in a beautiful framed drawing of a cute cartoon-like green dragon playing with a little cartoon rabbit (she said this was her) holding a toy wooden sword with a cooking pot on its head.

In the drawing, the dragon was touching the end of the sword with its front paw and the caption said "Ooh! Sharp!" The pain was still much bigger than her, but the playfulness and friendliness was evident. She gave me that drawing and I keep it in my office to remind myself and others of the possibilities when we can make peace with our pain and choose to thrive.

You can choose to complete your journey!

I have been fortunate to be a guide and coach for many people on their journey to freedom from suffering and have seen most of them get to this thriving stage. Unfortunately, there were some who got stuck on the journey or just quit trying. Some of the ones who quit did come back to me or other helpers and eventually completed their journey; but unfortunately, some died during the trek. If you are willing to do the footwork, you can be one of the people who thrive and cruise to the finish line and then begin to enjoy the rest of your life.

The Only Limits Are Your Own Willingness and Motivation

Willingness

A key ingredient for freedom from suffering is your own willingness to do whatever it takes to improve your quality of life and pain management. Many of the people I've worked with were burned out with trying over and over to find the quick fix—or in many cases any fix—for their chronic pain management.

Some of my former patients were so depressed, tired of trying and of not obtaining effective pain management, they wanted to give up. Sometimes they would tell me "I don't want to keep going." My answer to them is that it's OK to not want to keep going; but are you willing to do it anyway? You don't even have to like it or want it but you just need to be willing to do it anyway. Don't be a victim. Don't give your power away.

You may face many times on your journey where you want to quit. That's normal. There may be times on your journey when you make mistakes or fail at something. That's also normal. Most successful people share that their greatest successes came after their biggest failures. In the movie *Batman Begins*, there was a line where Bruce Wayne's father tells him that when you fall down you pick yourself up and keep going. Many of my "mistakes" were my biggest learning opportunities. This can be true for you if you are willing. Willingness leads to improved motivation.

Motivation

Just willingness is not enough. You next need to get into action and that requires that you motivate yourself to keep going even when times get tough. In sports I always heard coaches say the classic motivational quote, "When the going gets tough; the tough get going." That actually became my mantra during my early rehabilitation process.

When I was in sports I had coaches to help motivate me. When I went into the Marine Corps I had officers to help motivate me. In karate I had my sensei (teacher) to really motivate me. When it came to pain management and physical rehabilitation I needed to find new coaches and guides to help keep me motivated. But most importantly, I needed to learn how to motivate myself—and so do you if you want to be successful on this journey to freedom from suffering.

It's Time to Write in Your Journal

Take a few minutes to write in your journal at this point. The first step is to start listing all the people you can call on to help keep you motivated. Then figure out what you believe each of them can say or do when they see you losing your willingness and motivation. What affirmation or slogan can you come up with to memorize and post in different places to remind you to stay willing and motivated?

Your Sixth Step Call to Action

You have now completed the sixth step of your pain management journey and here is your opportunity to summarize your experience in this step. Please answer the three questions below:

1. What is the most important thing you have learned about yourself and your pain management as a result of completing this step?

   _____

   _____

   _____

   _____

   _____

2. What are you willing to commit to do differently as a result of what you have learned by completing this step?

_____

_____

_____

_____

_____

_____

3. What obstacles might get in the way of your making these changes and what can you do to overcome those roadblocks?

_____

_____

_____

_____

_____

_____

**Please Take Time to
Pause, Rest, and Reflect
Then Go on to the Final Step**

Step Seven: The End of the Beginning

You are now on the final step and near the end of the beginning of thriving with chronic pain. In this step you will have the opportunity to finalize a new way of living that before beginning this journey you might not have believed possible. Of course you need to put into action all the new insights you have gathered on your passage from suffering to freedom.

In the next chapter you will have an opportunity to pull it all together and see how far you have really come. But before you get there you need to learn about the balance points for successful living and thriving with chronic pain.

The Five Balance Points for Successful Chronic Pain Management

To find a balance point you must be able to identify what the extremes are that you need to balance. In the list below you will see each of the five target balance points you need to strive to obtain in your life. In the remainder of this section you will see what the extremes of each point are and why it is important to find the healthy balance point in each of the five areas.

- Positive Self-Talk
- Appropriate Emotional Expression
- Healthy Support Network
- Spirituality/Humility
- Effective Pain Management

Most people pay little attention to all the random thoughts that go through their head each day. Unfortunately, this is not the best way to go through life if you want to thrive. Consider a quote attributed to the Dalai Lama that I've posted below.

> Watch your thoughts, for they become words. Choose your words, for they become actions. Understand your actions, for they become habits. Study your habits, for they will become your character. Develop your character, for it becomes your destiny.

Balance Point One: Positive Self-Talk

The first balance point is *positive self-talk.* On one end of this continuum is *repressed self-talk.* When you are at this end of the spectrum you are not listening to your thoughts that eventually create your destiny. When your thoughts can lead you to making poor choices this might not be such a good thing. However, for the most part it is important to monitor your thinking patterns so you can end up not creating negative consequences for yourself.

At the other end of this balance point is *negative self-talk.* You covered some of this type of thinking earlier when you learned about anticipatory pain and pain versus suffering. Another way this plays out for people living with chronic pain is the negative thinking can worsen depression or self-hatred. Both ends of this spectrum put you at risk of hurting yourself. Some people hurt themselves by trying to medicate this condition while others go for the long-term solution to a short-term problem—suicide.

The premise for striving for this *positive self-talk* balance point is: if you change how you think, it will start changing how you feel. If you can change how you think and feel, it will change the decisions you make and the actions you take. If you change your behaviors to more positive habits and make them habitual, you will feel better about yourself and obtain a more positive way of life—your destiny. Some people need to start by thinking their way into positive behaviors while others might need to behave their way into healthier thinking—I recommend doing both.

Balance Point Two: Appropriate Emotional Expression

A trap I see some people fall into is labeling feelings or emotions as either good or bad. I do not believe in "good" or "bad" emotions. I do believe that many emotions can, however, be comfortable or uncomfortable. Some emotions such as happiness or joy are sought after, while other emotions like fear or loneliness are to be avoided at all costs. This type of paradigm can lead to going to one dangerous end or the other of this spectrum.

As with the first balance point *appropriate emotional expression* also has a continuum of extremes. One end of the spectrum is becoming *emotionally numb*. For some people this numbness is chemically enhanced or induced. But for most people the numbness is more of an acquired defense mechanism due to a constant barrage of living with extremely uncomfortable emotions in addition to high levels of physical chronic pain. This numbness can lead to pushing friends and loved ones away or becoming hopeless. You saw the dangers of hopelessness in the previous step.

Then there is the other extreme—*emotional overreaction*. The example I like for this is to imagine being in a situation that triggers anger. The trigger might be getting cut off in traffic or having someone cut in front of you when waiting in a line for services. For most people this might trigger two pounds of emotional response—getting mad or frustrated. Unfortunately, people at this end of the spectrum might react with twenty pounds of pressure—rage or even blind rage. So it is with other uncomfortable emotions like fear, sadness, loneliness, and anxiety.

Another problem with this balance point is that some people can vacillate between the two extremes and never stop at the balance point. The first step toward *appropriate emotional expression* is being able to recognize, articulate and rate your emotions. Once this is accomplished the next step is learning how to appropriately express your emotions. Making better choices on what to say and do when you experience emotions, especially strong uncomfortable emotions, will lead to much more positive outcomes for you and those around you. Below is an example of a feeling checklist to help you put words to your emotions (circle one on each line) and rate the intensity on a 1–10 scale.

Strong	or	Weak?	Intensity = _____
Caring	or	Angry?	Intensity = _____
Happy	or	Sad?	Intensity = _____
Safe	or	Threatened?	Intensity = _____
Fulfilled	or	Frustrated?	Intensity = _____
Proud	or	Ashamed?	Intensity = _____
Connected	or	Lonely?	Intensity = _____
Peaceful	or	Agitated?	Intensity = _____

Balance Point Three: Healthy Support Network

You have seen many times in this book the importance of building a chronic pain support network for yourself. This balance point of a *healthy support network* also has two dangerous extremes—isolation and enabling. Let's start with the *isolation* extreme. This is usually fueled with the belief that I have to do it myself. Sometimes this is coming from a power position because of a mistaken belief like, "I can't trust or depend on others." While for other people the mistaken belief might be, "I have to do it myself because I'm no good; or nobody is there for me." Either way you lose the chance to have someone in your corner when it really counts.

The other end of this continuum is enabling. Some people at this end have developed a system of "support" where they overly depend on others—even when they can and should be doing things for themselves. The denial pattern of *fear of change*, usually leads to this type of system. I've seen some of my patients recognize this and want to change and gain their power back and the old enabling support system goes crazy. The enablers are also stuck in the fear of change defense pattern. Again, that is why you have had many opportunities in this book to learn about building a *healthy support network*.

People are not enabling you if you really do need support in achieving a goal and you do not in fact have the ability or means to do it by yourself. You need to do this freedom journey *for* yourself—but not *by* yourself. It takes a collaborative team approach to obtain the best pain management plan. This team must be comprised of professional healthcare people along with other guides and coaches in order for you to obtain true freedom from suffering and move on to thriving.

Balance Point Four: Spirituality/Humility

The next balance point of spirituality/humility also has problematic extremes. Here, too, people can vacillate between the extremes and never stay in the middle. On one end of the spectrum people are at risk for moving into pride and/or arrogance while at the opposite end is shame and guilt.

As you learned in step two of this book, spirituality is a complex and multidimensional part of the human experience. It involves beliefs, perceptions, thinking, feeling, experiential and behavioral aspects. The thinking or belief and perception aspects include the search for meaning, purpose, and truth in life and the beliefs and values by which a person lives their life. The experiential and emotional aspects involve feelings of hope, love, connection, inner peace, comfort, and support. The behavioral aspects of spirituality involve the way a person externally demonstrates their individual spiritual beliefs and inner spiritual state.

When people are at either end they close themselves off to the spiritual energy that will enhance their quality of life and improve their pain management. When in pride or arrogance the mistaken belief is *I am in control.* Sometimes that can be a good thing; however, when people mistakenly believe they are in control when they really aren't they can experience a lot of trauma and drama in their lives as well as pain and suffering. False pride, or arrogance, also keeps you from reaching out to others for appropriate and healthy support.

The other end of the spectrum has its own negative consequences if you get stuck in *shame and guilt.* I believe that healthy shame and appropriate guilt have a place in our lives. The problem I'm talking about here is toxic shame and dysfunctional or paralyzing guilt. Healthy shame lets us know we have limits. Toxic shame leads us to seek dangerous cover-ups to cope with it. Appropriate guilt lets us know when our behavior needs modification. Dysfunctional guilt leads us to becoming overresponsible and accepting blame that we really don't merit. In addition, shame and guilt also keep us from reaching out to others.

Balance Point Five: Effective Pain Management

This last balance point of *effective pain management* is what this book is all about. The two extremes here are *ignor-*

ing pain or *suffering*. I believe there are times when ignoring pain—or avoidance by healthy appropriate distraction—can be a good thing. I don't believe it is ever a good thing to be in suffering from your pain as we covered in-depth earlier in step three.

Ignoring pain becomes a problem when you are not listening to what your pain is trying to tell you. When you're not listening it is impossible to take appropriate action. In fact, ignoring pain will often lead to suffering—sometimes quickly and sometimes it may take a while. One common reason many people ignore their pain is the mistaken belief that if I ignore my pain, it will go away. Another reason is that sometimes your ignoring the pain is because you don't know what else to do about it. This can easily lead to the stuck point of becoming hopeless that you learned about in the previous chapter.

Looking Forward: Planning the Next Steps on Your Journey

As the title of this step states, this is just the end of the beginning of your lifelong journey of thriving with chronic pain and refusing to suffer ever again. The first few years of my pain management journey were full of pain and suffering. I can honestly say I have NOT suffered with my pain for the past twenty-eight years.

How do I do that? I practice what I teach—even when I don't want to. In order to maintain my freedom from suffering I have to continuously and consistently be vigilant about identifying and managing stuck points as well as working to maintain balance at all five of the balance points identified earlier. That means I have to keep improving my biological fitness, psychological balance, social commitments, and spiritual development. Do I do it perfectly? Of course not! I believe in the premise of "progress not perfection."

Please gather as much insight as possible in the call to

action section of this step and the pulling it all together section. Then in the final call to action chapter you will be asked one last time to make a commitment to keep growing. Remember, we are either going up or going down—you can't stand still and achieve freedom from suffering.

Your Seventh Step Call to Action

It is time to sum up what you learned so far now that you have come to the end of this seventh and final step on your pain management journey. Please answer the three questions below.

1. What is the most important thing you learned about yourself and your pain management as a result of completing this step?

_____

_____

_____

2. What are you willing to commit to do differently as a result of what you learned by completing this step?

_____

_____

_____

3. What obstacles might get in the way of your making these changes and what can you do to overcome those roadblocks?

_____

_____

_____

Please Take Time to Pause, Rest, and Reflect Then Go on to the Next Section to Pull it All Together

Pulling it All Together: You've Only Just Begun—But Look How Far You've Come

Now that you have almost completed this book it is time to rate yourself on how much you have accomplished by completing the seven strategic steps to freedom from suffering. You will be scoring yourself on a 0 to 10 scale with 0 meaning you didn't achieve anything in that step and 10 meaning you got the most possible. Don't worry if your score is low; you can always bring it up. But don't get complacent if you score high because without ongoing action it will most certainly go down.

The healing process is like walking up a down escalator.
If you stop or stand still, you will go down.

- **Step One—It's Time to Wake Up:** How much did you learn about some of the common factors that may have kept you in a chronic pain trance? How well do you understand the role of depression and denial and how your thoughts, feelings, and behaviors can negatively impact you on bad pain days? How did you do on developing a depression management plan and discovering ways to get out of that problem and start breaking the chronic pain trance? And most important, how well did you accomplish your call to action for this step?

  Please Select Achievement Level:

  0   1   2   3   4   5   6   7   8   9   10

233

- **Step Two—Taking a Fresh Look at Your Relationship with Pain:** How well do you understand the pain system and the biological, psychological, and social components of chronic pain? What did you learn about addressing pain management at three essential levels and understanding three of the roadblocks—anxiety, trauma, and sleep problems? And most important, how well did you accomplish your call to action for this step?

  Please Select Achievement Level:
  0   1   2   3   4   5   6   7   8   9   10

- **Step Three—Exploring Pain versus Suffering:** How well did you learn that you can change your perception of pain and learn to cope with anticipatory pain? How well did you learn to decrease your levels and perception of pain and rating the severity of your pain, as well as determining the difference between the physical and psychological/emotional components of your pain? And most important, how well did you accomplish your call to action for this step?

  Please Select Achievement Level:
  0   1   2   3   4   5   6   7   8   9   10

- **Step Four—Exploring Effective Pain Management:** How well did you learn better ways to get your pain management needs met? How well do you understand the three core components of an effective pain management plan and how to start developing your own personal proactive plan? And most important, how well did you accomplish your call to action for this step?

  Please Select Achievement Level:
  0   1   2   3   4   5   6   7   8   9   10

- **Step Five—To Medicate or Not to Medicate—That *Is* the Question:** Were you able to take an honest and hard look at the medication management component of your pain management plan? How well do you understand the definitions of tolerance, dependence, pseudoaddiction, and addiction and how to identify any potential red flags or medication management problems you may be experiencing now or in the future? And most important, how well did you accomplish your call to action for this step?

Please Select Achievement Level:
0   1   2   3   4   5   6   7   8   9   10

- **Step Six—Overcoming Five Stuck Points to Achieving Full Freedom:** How well do you understand the importance of identifying and managing the five stuck points that could sabotage your journey? How well did you learn how to transition successfully through your obstacles to freedom? And most important, how well did you accomplish your call to action for this step?

Please Select Achievement Level:
0   1   2   3   4   5   6   7   8   9   10

- **Step Seven—The End of the Beginning:** How well do you understand and how well are you implementing the five balance points for effective pain management? How well did you pull everything you have learned together and start to develop a plan for the next stage of your journey to stay free from suffering? And most important, how well did you accomplish your call to action for this step?

Please Select Achievement Level:
0   1   2   3   4   5   6   7   8   9   10

Your Final Call to Action

This is the final step of your new pain management journey; it's now time to evaluate what you have learned so far and develop a plan to move forward. Please answer the questions below and share your answers with someone you trust. It can be very helpful to share your answers with everyone on your new pain management team.

1. Please list each of your call to action commitments you completed for each of the seven steps of this book below:

    _____

    _____

    _____

    _____

    _____

    _____

    _____

    _____

    _____

    _____

    _____

    _____

2. As you review each of the action steps in Question 1, what is the most important thing you have learned about yourself and your pain management journey as a result of completing this book?

    _____

    _____

    _____

    _____

    _____

    _____

    _____

_____

_____

_____

_____

_____

_____

3. What are you willing to commit to do differently as a result of what you have learned by completing this book? This is in addition to your earlier action steps above.

_____

_____

_____

_____

_____

_____

_____

4. What obstacles might get in the way of your making these changes and what can you do to overcome those potential roadblocks?

_____

_____

_____

_____

_____

_____

_____

5. Who are you going to share your answers with and how can they support you and help hold you accountable to your commitment to action?

_____

_____

_____

_____

_____

_____

_____

_____

_____

Appendix

About the Author

Dr. Stephen F. Grinstead, LMFT, ACRPS, CADC-II

Dr. Grinstead is the Clinical Director of Training and Consultation for the Gorski-CENAPS® Corporation. He is also an author and internationally recognized expert in preventing relapse related to chronic pain disorders and is the developer of the Addiction-Free Pain Management® System (please visit *www.addiction-free.com* for more information). He has been working with pain management, chemical addictive disorders, eating addiction, and coexisting mental and personality disorders for nearly 30 years.

Dr. Grinstead has a bachelor's degree in behavioral science, a master's degree in counseling psychology, and a doctorate in addictive disorders. He is a Licensed Marriage and Family Therapist (LMFT), a California Certified Alcohol and Drug Counselor (CADC-II), and an Advanced Relapse Prevention Specialist (ACRPS). He was on the faculty of the University of California, Santa Cruz, Alcohol and Drug Studies Program and also taught at Santa Clara University; University of California, Berkeley; and Stanford University Medical School. He is currently on the faculty of the University of Utah's School on Alcoholism and Other Drug Dependencies.

Since 1996, Dr. Grinstead has conducted *Addiction-Free Pain Management®, Managing Pain Medication in Recovery, Managing Pain and Prescription Drug Abuse, Relapse Prevention Counseling, Relapse Prevention for Eating Addiction,* and *Denial Management Counseling* seminars and certification trainings for well over fifteen thousand healthcare professionals and therapists at more than 180 training seminars in key cities across the United States and Canada. He has also developed and presented several other addiction-related trainings including: *HIV/AIDS and Chemical Dependency, Domestic Violence and Chemical Dependency,* and *Recovery and Relapse Prevention for Eating Addiction.*

Dr. Grinstead has authored and co-authored books and pamphlets with Terence T. Gorski, president of the Gorski-CENAPS® Corporation, including the following publications.

Dr. Grinstead's Publications

Addiction-Free Pain Management® Recovery Guide: Managing Pain and Medication in Recovery, (2nd ed., 2008)

Addiction-Free Pain Management®—The Professional Guide (out of print)

Addiction-Free Pain Management: Relapse Prevention Counseling Workbook, (revised 2007)

APM Module One: Understanding and Evaluating Your Chronic Pain Symptoms

APM Module Two: Examining Your Potential Medication Management Problems

APM Module Three: Understanding and Developing Effective Pain Management

APM Module Four: A Guide for Managing Pain Medication in Recovery

Denial Management Counseling for Effective Pain Management Workbook: Practical Exercises for Motivating People in Chronic Pain toward More Effective Pain Management

Denial Management Counseling Professional Guide: Advanced Clinical Skills for Motivating Substance Abusers to Recover

Denial Management Counseling Workbook: Practical Exercises for Motivating Substance Abusers to Recover

Managing Pain and Coexisting Disorders: Using the Addiction-Free Pain Management™ System

Recovery and Relapse Prevention for Food Addiction Workbook (out of print)

Relapse Prevention Therapy Workbook: Identifying Early Warning Signs Related to Personality and Lifestyle Problems, (revised 2010)

The Eating Addiction Relapse Prevention Workbook: For Compulsive Overeaters, Binge Eaters, and Food Addicts

Pain Management Bibliography and Recommended Reading List

Barrett, S., et al. (2006). *Consumer Health: A Guide to Intelligent Decisions.* Columbus, OH: McGraw-Hill.

Boriskin, J. (2004). *PTSD and Addiction: A Practical Guide for Clinicians and Counselors.* Center City, MN: Hazelden.

Campbell, J., et al. (2006). *Emerging Strategies for the Treatment of Neuropathic Pain.* Seattle, WA: International Association for the Study of Pain (IASP) Press.

Carr, D., Loeser, J., & Morris, D. Narrative, pain, and suffering. *Progress in Pain Research and Management 2005, 34.* Seattle, WA: International Association for the Study of Pain (IASP) Press.

Catalano, E., & Hardin, K. (1996). *The Chronic Pain Control Workbook: A Step-by-Step Guide for Coping with and Overcoming Pain,* (2nd ed.). Oakland, CA: New Harbinger Publications.

Caudill, M. (2001). *Managing Pain before it Manages You.* New York, NY: Guilford Press.

Chino, A., & Davis, C. (2000). *Validate Your Pain: Exposing the Chronic Pain Cover-up.* Stanford, FL: Health Access Press.

Cleveland, M. (1999). *Chronic Illness and the Twelve Steps: A Practical Approach to Spiritual Resilience.* Center City, MN: Hazelden.

Colvin, R. (2002). *Prescription Drug Addiction: The Hidden Epidemic.* Omaha, NE: Addicus Books.

Corey, D., & Solomon, S. (1989). *Pain: Free Yourself for Life.* New York, NY: Penguin Books USA.

Davis, M., Eshelman, E. R., & McKay, M. (1995). *The Relaxation & Stress Reduction Workbook,* (4th ed.). Oakland, CA: New Harbinger Publications.

Deardorff, W. (2004). *The Psychological Management of Chronic Pain.* ContinuingEdCourses.Net: *www.continuingedcourses.net.*

Deardorff, W., & Reeves, J. (1997). *Preparing for Surgery: A Mind-Body Approach to Enhance Healing and Recovery.* Oakland, CA: New Harbinger Publications.

Egoscue, P. (1998). *Pain Free: A Revolutionary Method for Stopping Chronic Pain.* New York, NY: Bantam Books.

Ford, N. (1994). *Painstoppers: The Magic of All-Natural Pain Relief.* West Nyack, NY: Parker Publishing Company, Inc.

Fuhr, A. Activator methods chiropractic technique: The science and art. *Today's Chiropractic 1995* (July/August), 48–52.

Gatchel, R. & Turk, D. (1996). *Psychological Approaches to Pain Management.* New York/London: Guilford Press.

Gorski, T. (2010). *Straight Talk about Suicide.* Independence, MO: Herald House/Independence Press.

Gorski, T. (2006). *Depression and Relapse: A Guide to Recovery.* Independence, MO: Herald House/Independence Press.

Gorski, T. & Grinstead, S., (2010). *Relapse Prevention Therapy Workbook: Updated, Revised, and Simplified.* Independence, MO: Herald House/Independence Press.

Gorski, T. & Grinstead, S., (2006). *Denial Management Counseling Workbook,* (rev. ed.). Independence, MO: Herald House/Independence Press.

Gorski, T., & Grinstead, S. (2000). *Denial Management Counseling Professional Guide.* Independence, MO: Herald House/Independence Press.

Grant, M. (2001). *Pain Control with EMDR: An Information Processing Approach.* (2nd ed.). Oakland, CA: New Harbinger Publications, Inc.

Grinstead, S. (2008). *Addiction-Free Pain Management® Re-*

covery Guide: Managing Pain and Medication in Recovery, (2nd ed.). Independence, MO: Herald House/Independence Press.

Grinstead, S. (2007). *Managing Pain and Coexisting Disorders: Using the Addiction-Free Pain Management® System.* Independence, MO: Herald House/Independence Press.

Grinstead, S., Gorski, T., & Corbitt, S. (2007). *Eating Addiction: The Relapse Prevention Workbook.* Independence, MO: Herald House/Independence Press.

Grinstead, S., Gorski, T., & Messier J. (2006). *Denial Management Counseling for Effective Pain Management.* Independence, MO: Herald House/Independence Press.

Grinstead, S. & Gorski, T. (2006). *Addiction-Free Pain Management®: Relapse Prevention Counseling Workbook,* (rev. ed.). Independence, MO: Herald House/Independence Press.

Grinstead, S. & Gorski, T. (1999). *Addiction-Free Pain Management®: The Professional Guide.* Independence, MO: Herald House/Independence Press.

Kennedy, J., & Crowley, T. (1990). Chronic pain and substance abuse: A pilot study of opioid maintenance. *Journal of Substance Abuse Treatment, 7*(4), 233–238.

Khalsa, D. & Stauth, C. (2002). *Meditation as Medicine: Activate the Power of Your Natural Healing Force.* New York, NY: Fireside.

Kingdon, R., Stanley, K. & Kizior, R. (1998). *Handbook for Pain Management.* Philadelphia, PA: W. B. Saunders.

Meade, T., et al. (1995). Randomized comparison of chiropractic and hospital outpatient management for low back pain: Results from extended follow-up. *British Medical Journal, 311,* 349–351.

Melzack, R. and Wall, P. (1965). Pain mechanisms: A new theory. *Science, 150,* 971–979.

Melzack, R. and Wall, P. (1982). *The Challenge of Pain.* New York, NY: Basic Books.

Merskey, H., Loeser, J., & Dubner, R., (Eds.) (2005). *The Paths of Pain: 1975–2005.* Seattle WA: International Association for the Study of Pain (IASP) Press.

Osterbauer, P., et al. (1992). Three-dimensional head kinematics and clinical outcome of patients with neck injury treated with manipulative therapy: A pilot study. *Journal of Manipulative Physiological Therapy, 15*(8), 501–511.

Pinsky, D., et al. (2004). *When Painkillers Become Dangerous.* Center City, MN: Hazelden.

Reilly, R. (1993). *Living with Pain: A New Approach to the Management of Chronic Pain.* Minneapolis, MN: Deaconess Press.

Rogers, R., & McMillin, C. (1989). *The Healing Bond: Treating Addictions in Groups.* New York, NY: W. W. Norton & Company.

Rome, J., (2002). *Mayo Clinic on Chronic Pain,* (2nd ed.). Rochester, MN: Mayo Foundation for Medical Education and Research.

Rosenfeld, A., (2003). *The Truth about Chronic Pain: Patients and Professionals on How to Face it, Understand it, Overcome it.* New York, NY: Basic Books.

Roy, R. (1992). *The Social Context of the Chronic Pain Sufferer.* Toronto, Ontario, Canada: University of Toronto Press.

Sarno, J. (1991). *Healing Back Pain: The Mind-Body Connection.* New York, NY: Warner Books.

Sarno, J. (1998). *The Mindbody Prescription: Healing the Body, Healing the Pain.* New York, NY: Warner Books.

Stacy, C., Kaplan, A., & Williams, G. (1992). *The Fight Against Pain.* New York, NY: Consumers Union.

Stanford, M. (1998). *Foundations in Behavioral Pharmacology: For Social Workers, Psychologists, Therapists, and Counselors.* Santa Cruz, CA: Lightway Centre.

Stimmel, B. (1983). *Pain, Analgesia, and Addictions: The Pharmacologic Treatment of Pain.* New York, NY: Raven.

Stimmel, B. (1997). *Pain and its Relief without Addiction: Clini-*

cal Issues in the Use of Opioids and other Analgesics. New York, NY: Haworth Medical.

St. Marie, B. & Arnold, S., (Eds.), (2002). *When Your Pain Flares Up.* Minneapolis, MN: Fairview Press.

Tennant, F., Shannon J., Nork, J., Sagherian, A., & Berman, M. (1991). Abnormal adrenal gland metabolism in opioid addicts: Implications for clinical treatment. *Journal of Psychoactive Drugs, 23* (2), 135–149.

Turk, D., Rudy, T., & Sorkin, B. (1993). Neglected topics in chronic pain treatment outcome studies: Determination of success. *Pain, 53*(1), 3–16.

U.S. Department of Health and Human Services. Pain management without psychological dependence: A guide for healthcare providers. *Substance Abuse in Brief Fact Sheet, Summer 2006, 4*(1).

Vertosick, F. (2000). *Why We Hurt: The Natural History of Pain.* New York, NY: Harcourt.

Wall, P., & Jones, M. (1991). *Defeating Pain: The War Against the Silent Epidemic.* New York, NY: Plenum Publishing Corporation.

Warfield, C. (1996). *Expert Pain Management.* Spring House, PA: Springhouse Corporation.

Watkins, J., & Watkins, H. (1990). Dissociation and displacement: Where goes the ouch? *American Journal of Clinical Hypnosis, 33*(1), 1–10.

Young, M., & Baar, K. (2002). *Women and Pain: Why it Hurts and What You Can Do.* New York, NY: Hyperion Books.

Useful Internet Resources

Addiction-Free Pain Management®

www.addiction-free.com

Addiction-Free Pain Management® (APM) describes the treatment system developed by Dr. Stephen F. Grinstead to help people suffering with chronic pain who also have coexisting problems including addiction due to living with chronic pain.

Addiction No More

www.addictionnomore.com

Addiction No More offers drug and alcohol referrals to thousands of drug rehabilitation centers all over the United States and Canada.

American Academy of Pain Management

www.aapainmanage.org

The American Academy of Pain Management is the largest multidisciplinary pain society and largest physician-based pain society in the United States. The Academy is a nonprofit multidisciplinary credentialing society providing credentialing to practitioners in the area of pain management.

American Society of Addiction Medicine

www.asam.org

The nation's medical specialty society dedicated to educating physicians and improving the treatment of individuals suffering from alcoholism and other addictions, including those with pain and addiction.

American Society for Pain Management Nursing

www.aspmn.org

The American Society for Pain Management Nursing is an organization of professional nurses dedicated to promoting and providing optimal care of individuals with pain, including the management of its sequelae (resulting conditions). This is accomplished through education, standards, advocacy, and research.

Benson Henry Institute

www.massgeneral.org/bhi

The Benson Henry Institute is a world leader in the study, advancement, and clinical practice of mind/body medicine. You can find help if you're experiencing the negative effects of stress; learn how to elicit the relaxation response; review courses for health professionals; and sample a new line of relaxation CDs. Breathe deeply...exhale...and make the mind/body connection.

Body Mind Resources

www.bodymindresources.com

This site was founded to help keep people out of pain. Liam is a massage therapist and structural bodyworker with a mission to help and guide all those who are bold enough to begin the adventure of putting their bodies back together and getting out of pain.

Dancing with Pain

www.dancingwithpain.com

Dancing with Pain® offers educational seminars, movement workshops, and community forums that help individuals navigate through the world of chronic pain and discover natural pain relief.

Decision Maker® Institute/Lefkoe Institute

www.decisionmaker.com/dmi.htm

This site is the home of several processes that enable people to make radical changes in their behavior and feelings by quickly and permanently eliminating the beliefs that determine what they do and feel. It also has techniques that decondition the stimuli for such emotions as fear, anger, and guilt.

Drug Free At Last

www.drugfreeatlast.com

Selecting a drug rehab for yourself or someone you care

about is one of the most important decisions you will make. On this site you can find the right treatment for drug abuse. Their services are free to the public. This site also includes valuable information about many of the drugs of abuse.

Enhanced Healing through Relaxation Music

www.enhancedhealing.com

On this site you will find relaxation music, positive affirmations, and online counseling for reducing stress and anxiety, promoting health, wellness, and healing as well as improving self-esteem.

Gorski-CENAPS® Corporation

www.cenaps.com

The home of Terence T. Gorski and the CENAPS® Training Team. Visit here for information on training and consultation services for recovery and relapse prevention issues for addiction and the related mental disorders, personality disorders, and lifestyle problems.

Holistic Help

www.holistichelp.net

Life management and support for people living with chronic illness, chronic pain, or disability. This site also offers education, consultation, pamphlets, articles, and e-books.

International Association for the Study of Pain

www.iasp-pain.org

Founded in 1973, IASP brings together scientists, clinicians, healthcare providers and policy makers to stimulate and support the study of pain and to translate that knowledge into improved pain relief worldwide. Currently, IASP has more than 7,000 members from 126 countries and in 85 chapters.

Metropolitan Pain Management Consultants

www.pain-mpmc.com

MPMC specializes in injuries and disease of the back such as work-related injuries, persistent back pain before and after surgery, degenerative disc disease, spinal arthritis, disease of the facet joints, injury to muscles or ligaments or pinched nerves in the neck and back. We treat complex regional pain syndrome (RSD), peripheral neuropathy and pain associated with vascular conditions.

Mind Publications

www.mindpub.com

A noncommercial, 24–7, self-help and coaching site to assist you with personal, family, and relationship problems such as anger, anxiety, depression, jealousy, marriage troubles, and parenting issues. Also helps you cope with chronic illness or pain.

The National Center for Complementary and Alternative Medicine (NCCAM)

nccam.nih.gov

NCCAM is dedicated to exploring complementary and alternative healing practices in the context of rigorous science, training complementary and alternative medicine (CAM) researchers, and disseminating authoritative information to the public and professionals.

National Fibromyalgia Association (NFA)

www.fmaware.org

The National Fibromyalgia Association (previously known as the National Fibromyalgia Awareness Campaign) is a 501(c)(3) nonprofit organization whose mission is: To develop and execute programs dedicated to improving the quality of life for people with fibromyalgia.

National Institute on Chemical Dependence (NICD)

www.nicd.us

Articles and directories for: health and wellness, addiction, prevention, recovery, medical, mental health, social issues, research, education, spirituality, and family.

Prolotherapy

www.prolotherapy.org

This website offers a comprehensive description of the prolotherapy procedure and the many pain conditions it effectively treats.

Scripps McDonald Center

www.mcdonald-center.scripps.org

Scripps McDonald Center is a nationally recognized organization dedicated to treating alcohol and drug abuse. The center, located in La Jolla, California, provides a healing environment—people needing help and their families receive the tools and support they need to rebuild their lives.

Terence T. Gorski's Addiction Website

www.tgorski.com

Terence T. Gorski's addiction and clinical development website is designed to keep decision makers, program managers, and clinicians up-to-the-minute on new developments regarding the Gorski-CENAPS® Model of Treatment.

Valley Forge Medical Center Breakthrough Chronic Pain Program

www.vfmc.net

Valley Forge Medical Center in Norristown, Pennsylvania, became the first Addiction-Free Pain Management® Center of Excellence in 2009. In addition to addiction specific treatment, Valley Forge Medical Center (VFMC) offers "Break-through" Chronic Pain Management Services developed specifically for those patients suffering from co-occurring issues of chronic pain and substance abuse and/or addiction. Many of the VFMC staff have been trained by Dr. Grinstead in the *Addiction-Free Pain Management® System* and are implementing this model to provide positive outcomes for their chronic pain patients. You can reach them by calling toll-free (888) 539-8500.